Testim

"Just like my first conversation with Alison, this book read my mind – exactly as I knew it would! In the past, I worried about what people thought of me and battled with Impostor Syndrome. Alison helped me overcome my fears, freeing me to progress my career in ways I hadn't imagined. If you ever experience fear or anxiety, this book will reassure you that you're not alone and that you can succeed while worrying less. Since working with Alison, I haven't looked back!"

– Maria Jennings, Marketing and Brand Director, Professional services firm

"I'm sure I'm not the only person who has battled with feelings of anxiety and self-doubt in their career – fear of getting things wrong and not being able to meet your own and others' exacting expectations. Alison's brilliantly insightful book has helped me understand the reasons behind these feelings and appreciate just how much impact our physical bearing has on our minds. She shares strategies to better equip me for challenging situations while giving me plenty of space to reflect and find an approach that works for me. I am certainly going to be making more use of my Genius Lounge in future!"

– Rebecca Rossiter, Director, Professional services firm

"Get a pen and paper ready to make copious notes for your journey to confident leadership! Alison has expertly spotlighted the emotions that can derail us as we progress to leadership roles. Reading this book was as though Alison had access to my feelings over the last few years and captured them on paper, along with great techniques to deal with them. If I'd had access to them before, I would have had fewer sleepless nights!"

– **Andy Noble, Managed Services Director, NTT UK&I Ltd**

"Alison's wealth of expertise comes to life in this thought-provoking and easy read. The strategies she shares are clear and practical – and they work! I found myself thinking through challenges in my head while reading, and now feel I'm more prepared and confident to tackle them."

– **Lauren McKenzie-Wilson, Director, Big Four accounting firm**

"I wish I'd read this book when I started my career. It would have saved me 20 years of anguish! Alison quickly and expertly guides you through the process of navigating your fears and doubts so you can unleash your leadership and bring the best of you to what you do."

– **Jen Brown, Performance & Wellbeing Coach**

"If you feel something is holding you back but can't quite put your finger on it, you'll likely find this book very helpful. In a fun way, it explains why we do what we do by delving into evolution, neuroscience and modern psychology to make sense of behaviours that get in our way. Although most examples are from the world of work, the practical and achievable steps teach you how to develop confidence for any situation."

– **David Harney, Senior manager, Cisco Systems**

"This book is a fantastic toolbox to help overcome daily stress and anxiety. It explains why we react the way we do in stressful situations, coupled with practical strategies to help overcome our fears. I particularly like the focus on challenging our current thinking to shift to a positive mindset. This is definitely a book I will turn to regularly on my leadership journey."

– **Bhavini Pandya, Senior manager,**
Big Four accounting firm

"Have you ever felt you're not ready to be a leader and want to change that? With a friendly and engaging style, Alison provides insights into what holds us back from fulfilling our true potential, with a good balance of stories, research and tools. I now have some useful tips that will transform the way I think about myself. Practising these techniques will help you silence the voice in your head and change the way you show up and lead. Highly recommended."

– **Laura Perretta, Global HR Director, Kantar**

"Alison provides deep insight – and a plan – to bring your best self to situations where you thought your best self would never show up. I experienced a delightful sense of familiarity and optimism as I read this book and appreciated Alison's empathy and authenticity. She combines real-world examples with literary and pop culture references, all supported by scientific research and evidence. It felt as if this book was written specifically for, and about, me though it's clearly for anyone looking for a compass to navigate towards feeling and being their best self."

– **Darren Daly, Service Operations Manager, NTT UK&I Ltd**

"We can all be hijacked by fear, taken off course from what we want and choose what fear wants instead. This book is a great, practical guide based on sound research that would help any executive maximise their performance."

– **Dr Amy Silver, Speaker, Mentor, Author of best seller, *The Loudest Guest: How to change and control your relationship with fear***

"This book has highlighted for me that fear is part and parcel of career progression, and we need to learn how to work with it. Alison shares detailed processes supported with real-life stories, walking you through tools you can apply in everyday situations to help you live and work at your best. Plenty here to learn from Alison. Be ready to tag your favourite pages!"

– **Dipti Thakrar, Country Tax Manager, Hitachi Powergrids**

Unleash Your Leadership

Unleash
Your
Leadership

How to worry less and achieve more

Alison Reid

Alison Reid

Published by Alison Reid

First published in 2021 in Great Britain.

All enquiries should be made to the author.

Edited by Jenny Magee

Typeset in Australia by BookPOD

Printed by Ingram Spark

ISBN: 978-1-8384148-0-1 (paperback)

ISBN: 978-1-8384148-1-8 (e-book)

To Mum and Dad, who were always there for me.

Dad once said he'd like to understand what I
did – maybe this book would have helped.

I miss you both.

Contents

Introduction   1

One: The F Word   9

Two: Your Journey to Confidence   17

Three: Why Evolution Has a Lot to Answer For   33

Four: Master Your Mind   49

Five: Harness Your Body   75

Six: Speak Your Voice   99

Seven: A Three-Step Process   115

Afterword   137

References   141

About the Author   151

Introduction

Does this sound familiar?

You're stressed out trying to keep on top of everything at work. Everyone wants a piece of you, but you feel unable to push back without it reflecting badly on you.

You're terrified of being put on the spot in meetings with Very Senior People. What if they ask about something outside your area of expertise and you don't know the answer?

You worry a lot about what people think of you. To be honest, you can't quite work out how you've got promoted this far. Surely you're going to get found out at some point?

You avoid difficult conversations with people because you're afraid of conflict. You suffer in silence and work around Problem People.

You don't think you're cut out for leadership. You think you need to be charismatic and inspiring and feel you don't fit the bill.

You're not alone!

As the professionals I work with gain seniority, I notice there's an expectation that they'll transition seamlessly from managing to leading. As though it's as simple as managing less and leading more.

They're expected to drive strategic projects while keeping on top of the day-to-day and making the numbers.

They need to inspire and engage their team to peak performance, and cope with lack of resource.

They're required to share their opinions and insights with senior stakeholders while ensuring they're grounded in data.

They need to build relationships, but they're stuck in back-to-back meetings.

Their managers often seem baffled as to why they don't just get on with it given their capability.

Yet although these individuals may seem outwardly confident, I find they're dogged with worry and anxiety. Like swans gliding on a lake, they're serene on the surface while paddling furiously underneath. As one recently promoted leader told me, *"I've wanted a seat at the leadership table for a long time but, now that I have it, I'm really struggling to make the shift from manager to leader."*

Imagine...

Let me take you into the future, perhaps a few months or a year from now, when things are different.

You feel confident and in control. Your team's doing a great job, freeing up more of your time to focus on strategic projects, business development and relationship-building.

You're in a meeting with Very Senior People. Despite the butterflies in your stomach, you're confident that you know what you're talking about and you're clear on the points you want to make. You're going to make them sit up and listen so you can get the decision you need.

You're interested in what other people think, but try not to dwell on their opinion of you. You know who you are and what's important.

You don't like to give people difficult messages – and still get nervous when you have to – but you know that it's for the best for them, the business, and you.

You're confident in yourself as a leader, sure that you can deal with anything that comes your way. You have a voice and know how to use it. You know where you want to make a difference and where to take your career to make that happen.

> You're worrying less and achieving more. You've unleashed your leadership.

You're worrying less and achieving more. You've unleashed your leadership.

How does it feel?

Create your future

The good news is that you can realise that imagined future. You have everything you need to be successful – you just need help to unlock it.

> You have everything you need to be successful – you just need help to unlock it.

This book will help you do exactly that.

It's about overcoming the fear and self-doubt that so often holds you back. It's about releasing the full force of your potential so you can achieve career success and lead yourself and others in service of what matters. Ultimately, it's about empowering and enabling you to unleash your leadership.

To help you do this, I'm going to:

- Explain the role of fear in human evolution and how it may be impacting your confidence and performance at work
- Offer practical strategies to help you manage worry, self-doubt and overthinking

- Talk about the importance of your body in how you think, feel and come across, and show you how to use it to increase your confidence and impact
- Help you prepare for and initiate "difficult" conversations
- Share a Three-Step Process to navigate challenging situations, bringing together everything you've learned.

Why can I help you?

I've been coaching managers and executives for nearly 20 years, helping them succeed in their current organisation or find success elsewhere. Over time, the questions I found myself asking most often in coaching sessions were, "What's holding you back from what you want?" and "What are you afraid of?" I realised the main barrier to individuals realising their career aspirations and leading themselves and others, isn't talent or skill – it's fear.

> The main barrier isn't talent or skill – it's fear.

This led me to research the role of fear in our evolution, how it shapes our behaviour and how it sabotages us as adults in our life and work. Most importantly, I've learned how to help people turn around fear-driven behaviours with practical strategies grounded in the latest neuroscience.

I care deeply about this topic because I also struggle with fear and self-doubt. At age seven, I was sent to a private girls' school. They achieved their goal of moulding me into a well-behaved, polished young lady, but, in the process, I learned that it wasn't ok to be me. A high-achiever, my confidence and self-worth became entangled with my performance – first at school, then in my career. Every sentence of this book has had to endure the harsh judgement of my inner critic. My fear of criticism means I'm an accomplished procrastinator and perfectionist.

To be honest, it's a miracle this book is in your hands!

How to use this book

This book is like a jigsaw puzzle. I'll be giving you pieces along the way that we'll put together at the end in the Three-Step Process. It's best read from front to back to start with, and I encourage you to take the time to pause when I suggest a reflection or exercise. After that, you can use it as a manual to refer to daily to help you deal with situations that arise – whether it's a negative thought that's bugging you or an imminent conversation or a meeting you're worried about.

Feel free to write in the book, underline ideas that resonate and tag pages that you want to come back to. The most important thing is that you practise the techniques. That's how you'll change the way you think and feel so you can move forward in your career with courage and confidence.

You can find more resources to support you at: www.alisonreid.co.uk/unleash-your-leadership/resources.

By the way, you'll find lots of stories throughout the book. These are from real people I've worked with in senior roles. To protect their identities, I've changed names and details. These stories will help you see you're not alone when dealing with confidence issues.

Are you ready? Then let's get started.

ONE

The F Word

Sam's story

I started working with Sam, an operations manager in a global technology company, when she'd been given the remit to restructure her team to improve efficiency and performance.

Her line manager approached me because she was frustrated that Sam wasn't executing the required changes quickly enough, and was concerned that Sam wasn't visible to key stakeholders. Sam's manager wanted her to be more decisive, more vocal, and proactive in getting buy-in.

When I spoke to Sam, it was clear she was feeling vulnerable and stressed. She felt under incredible pressure to meet expectations yet shackled by fear of failing. In particular:

- She didn't feel she had the confidence or the skills to execute the changes she needed to make – she didn't see herself as a leader.

- She felt exposed and fearful of the consequences of making a wrong step. She was paralysed with the fear of not doing the right thing.
- She wasn't reaching out to senior stakeholders to get buy-in for the planned restructure because she didn't feel important enough for them to give her the time of day.
- She spent a lot of time supporting her team – partly because they asked her and partly because she felt most comfortable in the day-to-day operations.

What's more, she said yes to everything and everyone because she didn't want to disappoint or be seen as difficult or not dedicated. She allowed meeting requests and her inbox to dictate her work. This meant that she was working long hours and wasn't getting to see her family enough. Especially tough with two toddlers at home.

Sam's experience illustrates three key challenges that so many of my clients struggle with. I wonder if you grapple with these too?

Swamped

As you take on more responsibility for managing people and projects, you find yourself navigating an increasing maelstrom of daily demands.

You're fielding requests from leadership, your colleagues, your team and, perhaps, your clients, and you're struggling to keep your head above the water. You feel you need to keep on top of everything or it will look as though you can't handle the responsibility.

You want to spend more time on strategic priorities, but there simply aren't enough hours in the day. What's more, you don't want to push back on work requests for fear of being judged as difficult and possibly damaging your career prospects. You also don't want to put more pressure on your team.

With people able to get hold of you on email, instant messaging and phone, it's like drinking from a firehose. And you don't feel you can turn the firehose off – you have to respond.

> With people able to get hold of you on email, instant messaging and phone, it's like drinking from a firehose.

One manager explained, *"I'm really stressed trying to keep on top of everything. I work very long hours, and it's affecting time with my family. I'm not sleeping well, and exercise has gone out of the window. When I'm not in back-to-back meetings, I'm trying to catch up with emails, and I'm not getting any of the important stuff done."*

Exposed

As you become more senior, situations arise where you're expected to have opinions and insights outside your subject matter expertise and make decisions without having all the facts. You feel exposed and fearful of saying or doing something wrong or stupid.

You don't have an issue with speaking with peers or more junior colleagues, but when you're in meetings with senior stakeholders (perhaps Partners or clients in a professional services firm or the executive team in a corporate), or you need to present to larger audiences, fear kicks in.

> As you become more visible in your organisation, you feel there's further to fall if you say or do something wrong.

When you **do** speak, you may be tentative in what you're saying. One manager received feedback from her line manager that, while she was regarded as a superstar, senior stakeholders perceived her as unsure of herself when it came to significant decisions. When the stakes were high, she didn't have conviction in her judgement calls.

And it's not just about speaking up. You hesitate to send certain emails and reports because you're afraid of making mistakes and being picked up on them. You hold back from reaching out to stakeholders to progress your project because you think they won't have time for you.

As you become more visible in your organisation, you feel there's further to fall if you say or do something wrong. You may have a mortgage and dependents to support, which means you feel even more worried about putting a foot wrong. And when you're working in a context of constant restructuring (the polite word for headcount reductions), this only exacerbates your anxiety.[1]

Torn

You've likely got where you are because you know what you're talking about, you're good at solving problems, and you're a good people manager. You get stuff done.

Yet as demands increase, you find you can no longer keep control of everything.

You may be reluctant to delegate more to your team – partly because you don't want to overload them, but also because you're worried they might make mistakes that will reflect poorly on you. Not only that, you may be avoiding tough conversations with your team members or colleagues about their performance or behaviour because you're afraid of the response you'll get.

There's something else I see going on here. One senior manager I worked with had trouble stepping back and allowing others to do the operational work. It can feel good to help people, especially your team – there's a real

> Embracing what it means to be a good leader means letting go of some of what it means to be a good manager.

sense of achievement from sorting out a problem.

Unfortunately, holding on to everything that makes you a good manager may be preventing you from creating bandwidth to contribute to shaping and growing the business, not just helping to run it. As one manager put it, she feels most comfortable "tinkering under the bonnet". But this isn't an option when you have a remit to lead change.

Embracing what it means to be a good leader means letting go of some of what it means to be a good manager.

The F word

In my experience, the underlying issue is fear – for Sam and so many of my clients.

Fear of being found out.

Fear of failure.

Fear of losing your reputation.

Fear of not being able to provide for your family.

Fear sounds a bit dramatic, doesn't it? It's more typical to talk about being stressed. However, stress is simply a physiological response to fear. We don't get stressed – we react to stressors in our environment. These can be anything from an overflowing inbox to a volatile boss to the threat of redundancy. In modern-day environments, we're often exposed continuously to stressors like these, which means we experience some level of fear or anxiety most of the time.

Fear sabotages leadership

A global survey of CEOs indicates that creativity and innovation are the most important skills for future leaders, yet they struggle to get enough of it in their organisations.[2]

However, when fear is at play – when, like Sam, you're afraid of getting it wrong, looking stupid, and losing your reputation – the last thing you'll be capable of is creativity and innovative thinking. Keeping your manager happy and not rocking the boat feels the safer option.

The coronavirus pandemic has only exacerbated the fear and anxiety that so many managers and leaders already experience.

What's next?

In the next chapter, we'll explore how fear shows up at work before mapping out how to unleash your leadership.

TWO

Your Journey to Confidence

How confident are you?

We all have different starting points in terms of our confidence level, and those points aren't necessarily fixed. Your degree of confidence may depend on where you're at in your career, or fluctuate depending on the situations you face. It's like standing on the rung of a ladder, then moving up or down depending on the circumstances.

So we'll start by identifying which rung is most familiar to you and then explore the resources that will help you move up.

> Your degree of confidence may depend on where you're at in your career, or fluctuate depending on the situations you face.

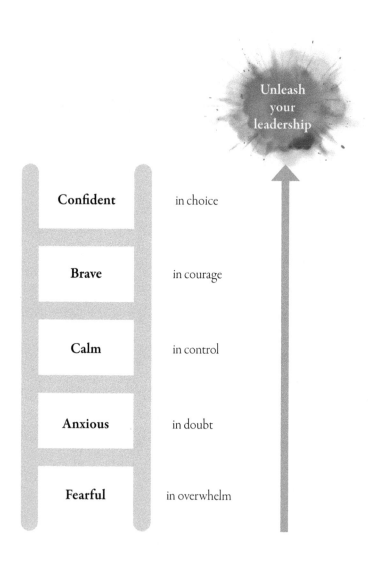

Figure 1: Confidence ladder

Fearful

*"Freedom from fear enables you
to do so much more."*

– Director, Third sector

On the bottom rung of the ladder, fear is paralysing you. You don't know what the right thing to do is and you're afraid of making a decision because you might fail. And that feels like a Really Big Deal.

Or you find yourself overcome by fear in high-stake situations – perhaps you get very nervous when presenting to senior stakeholders or even have a panic attack. It can feel as though your body has been taken over by an alien.

> It's like you're a small rowing boat buffeted about on an ocean in a big storm.

When you're fearful, you're in overwhelm, overpowered by negative thoughts and feelings. You're in survival mode, and it's difficult to think clearly. You find yourself making knee-jerk reactions to demands rather than taking time to respond.

It's like you're a small rowing boat buffeted about on an ocean in a big storm.

There's not much that's good about being here. Not making a decision may protect you from possible failure, but fear can also hijack your chances of positively impacting situations that matter.

So let's not hang around here – it's a little less bleak on the next rung of the ladder.

Anxious

"Anxiety is nothing but repeatedly experiencing failure in advance. What a waste."

– Seth Godin

Anxiety is still fear, but it's the diluted version. It's when you spend too much time worrying about what has or might happen, or what other people think of you.

Anxiety creates lots of mental noise. We often label it as self-doubt, and it tends to hold us back from speaking up and showing up. For example, Paul – recently promoted to a team leader role – is constantly worried about whether he's good enough for the job, and whether his line manager thinks he's up to the mark.

Anxiety can certainly drive performance and produce high standards. But the downside is that it can feed perfectionism and procrastination, increase stress, slow down productivity, and keep you from being seen and heard.

The good news is that you don't have to stick around here either. The next rung of the ladder, feeling calm, is within your reach. We just need to help you with techniques to manage negative thoughts and feelings so you can step up.

Calm

"Calm mind brings inner strength and self-confidence."

– The Dalai Lama

You can breathe now. You're feeling calm. The storm has abated, the sky is clear, and the sea is still, with just a whiff of a breeze to help you on your way.

When you're calm, you feel in control rather than being at the mercy of negative thoughts and feelings. You think and see clearly, and you're conscious and intentional about the best actions to take.

Calm allows you the space to choose whether and how to respond rather than just react. Even better, you're easier to be around and more open and approachable to colleagues and team members. Emotions are contagious, and that's a good thing when you're calm rather than fearful or anxious.

But calm isn't the final word when leading yourself and others. If you want to take a stand for what's important to you, you may need to speak up or take action. That means you may want to feel resolute or forceful instead.

However, courage works best when you're in command of your mind and body – grounded, not untethered.

Brave

> *"I learned that courage was not the*
> *absence of fear, but the triumph over it.*
> *The brave man is not he who does not feel*
> *afraid, but he who conquers that fear."*
>
> – Nelson Mandela

When you're brave, you're going beyond your comfort zone. You're doing things that make you feel anxious or fearful, such as sharing your opinion in a leadership meeting or saying no. You're in courage.

It doesn't mean you're not scared, but it's more painful to hold back than to say or do something. That's the moment when you gird your loins, walk on to the stage and take the microphone.

You need to keep on being brave to become stronger.

You need to keep on being brave to become stronger. The more you take courage, the more you expand your comfort zone, the more you see what you are capable of and build trust and belief in yourself: in other words, build your confidence.

Confident

"Once we believe in ourselves, we can risk curiosity, wonder, spontaneous delight, or any experience that reveals the human spirit."

– E.E. Cummings

When you're confident, it's as though you have an inner compass guiding your actions and decisions. You feel able to follow your own path rather than doing what you think others want or expect you to do. You're in choice. It doesn't mean that you won't face challenging situations and that things will be easy, but it does mean you trust that you have the resources to deal with whatever crosses your path. As one client said after we worked together, *"I now feel that there isn't a situation that's going to come up that I'm not going to be able to deal with."*

It's as though you're a mature oak tree, strongly rooted in the earth, stable enough to be unmoved except in the most ferocious of storms.

This is when you can truly lead.

When you're confident, it's as though you have an inner compass guiding your actions and decisions.

Dispelling the four myths about confidence

Myth One: You either have confidence, or you don't.

Certainly, some people are more confident than others. However, that doesn't mean you can't become confident. Neuroscience tells us that only 25-50 per cent of our confidence is genetic, which means that up to 75 per cent is up for grabs.[1]

Myth Two: Lack of confidence means a lack of competence.

It's not that competence isn't important, but, without it, competence isn't enough. One of the most consistent findings in psychology is the almost zero correlation between confidence and competence. There's minimal overlap between how good people are at something and how confident they are.[2]

The most confident people are sometimes the least competent because they don't know what they don't know. There's a fascinating example of this: a chap called Ferdinand Waldo Demara, also known as The Great Impostor. In the 1940s and 50s, he masqueraded as a surgeon, a professor and a prison warden. He even amputated a man's leg.[3]

Myth Three: It's simple.

Have you ever talked to someone about your lack of confidence and they've said something along the lines of, "You're great. You just need to have more confidence in yourself"?

If it was that simple, I'm sure you'd have nailed confidence a long time ago! Building confidence involves understanding and shifting long-held behavioural patterns through managing your mind, harnessing your body and taking courage to act in service of what you want. We can all do it, but it requires attention and practice.

Myth Four: It's a girl thing.

I've worked with plenty of men who suffer from self-doubt. Research has found that 50 per cent of women admit to experiencing self-doubt in their performance and careers, and 30 per cent of men do too.[4] I emphasise the word "admit" as men are less likely to admit to vulnerability.[5] However, there are differences in how men and women experience a lack of confidence, and I'll touch on these later.

What about you?

Where would you say you spend the most time on the ladder? Fearful, anxious, calm, brave or confident?

It may be that right now you're living in fear and anxiety, feeling panicky and overwhelmed. Or perhaps you feel calm and confident a lot of the time but fall off a cliff when faced with situations such as presenting to the board. It can feel like a game of snakes and ladders where you get all the way up only to slither down.

No matter how often you're experiencing fear and anxiety, I want to help you build your capacity to be calm and brave, so you develop an innate sense of confidence. I want you to trust yourself.

From fear to confidence

This isn't just a matter of getting from A to B. It's a journey.

You may be familiar with *The Hero's Journey* popularised by American professor and author, Joseph Campbell.[6] Even if you aren't, you will likely have seen it play out in umpteen movies and books. In summary, it's where a hero goes on an adventure or quest, leaving their familiar world behind. They face trials and tribulations as they navigate new and unfamiliar lands, a catalyst for personal learning and growth, and return home enlightened.

The Lord of the Rings is a good example. Wise wizard, Gandalf, asks the hobbit, Frodo, to go on a journey with a ring which has extraordinary powers. Frodo faces many challenges and often doubts he's up to the task. However, through his experiences, he grows in courage and confidence and takes sole responsibility for the mission to destroy the evil ring.[7]

> Your journey to confidence means deciding that it's more painful to hide than to put your head above the parapet.

Your journey to confidence means deciding that it's more painful to hide than to put your head above the parapet. It means battling with the gremlins that hold you back from saying and doing what you want. It means doing what Campbell calls "crossing the threshold" to do things that scare you. It means facing your fears to emerge a stronger person on the other side.

Resources for your journey

In *The Hero's Journey*, there's a point near the beginning where a guide or mentor appears and often gives the hero one or more talismans or artefacts to help them in their quest. For example, the Elf-queen gave Frodo The Phial of Galadriel to light up dark places.

That's where this book comes in. While I'm not in the talisman or artefacts business, I want to equip you with the essential resources for your journey to confidence. However, the twist here is that you already have the resources you need – I'm just here to help you access them. And those resources are your mind, your body and your voice.

Master your mind

"You have power over your mind. Realise this, and you will find strength."

– Marcus Aurelius

Before going backpacking for the first time, I had to make some tough decisions about what not to take in my pack. Apart from limited space, I needed to be able to lift and carry it!

> I want you to be the master of your mind, not a slave to it.

Our mind can be like that overladen backpack, so full of stuff that it weighs us down and stops us moving forward. Stuff such as negative thoughts, ingrained beliefs (the limiting type not the good ones) and unhelpful stories about how the world is.

And when we're anxious, negative thinking can gather momentum. It's as if our mind is a puppet-master, pulling our strings.

To help you on your journey, I need you to battle those inner gremlins that stop you saying and doing the things that are important to you.

The first resource to explore is your mind. We're going to:

- Look closely at what's going on in your head and why
- Examine how to deal with negative thoughts and nurture positive ones
- Introduce the idea that you can't master your mind without harnessing your body.

I want you to be the master of your mind, not a slave to it.

Harness your body

"Mr Duffy lived a short distance from his body."

– James Joyce

Your body isn't just going to be a carthorse on this journey. It's key to both your state of mind and your influence and impact as you deal with the challenges ahead.

> Your body isn't just going to be a carthorse on this journey.

We're going to:

- Put your body back on the proverbial map
- Explore the relationship between your body and how you think, feel and act
- Equip you with techniques to feel more calm, courageous and confident.

Speak your voice

"There's a moment when you have to choose whether to be silent or to stand up."

– Malala Yousafzai

In Campbell's journey, crossing the threshold is where the hero has to do things that scare them in order to carry on. That's where speaking up comes into play. In your world, it might be speaking up in a meeting, speaking out on unacceptable behaviour or saying no to someone.

Speaking up can be scary.

Speaking up can be scary. You might feel unsafe, afraid of looking stupid, or worried that you might upset someone or get into an argument. Yet unless you speak up for what you care about, you'll feel frustrated and resentful, and you won't be heard. You won't be able to influence what's important to you, while others carry on regardless.

We're going to look at:

- The situations where you may be finding it hard to speak up and why
- What you want to say and why it's important to you
- How to summon the courage to speak your voice.

Bringing it all together

Once we've done a deep-dive into the three resources, I'll share a process that brings them all together to help you get better outcomes in challenging situations, whether that's pressing send on an email or presenting at the executive forum.

Managers and executives I've worked with over many years have found this process powerful in overcoming fear and self-doubt, and increasing their confidence, influence and impact.

We'll explore:

- Why **awareness** is the first step to change and where David Attenborough comes into it
- The importance of **designing** a new behaviour that harnesses your mind, body and voice
- Why **practising** new behaviours is so important and what effective practice looks like

Before we delve into all that, it's important to understand why human beings are perfectly designed to lack confidence.

To do that, we're going to go back in time...

THREE

Why Evolution Has a Lot to Answer For

It's not confidence that's kept us alive – it's fear

Have you noticed that when you touch a worm, it wriggles away or curls up? The earthworm embodies nature's earliest attempt at a nervous system about 600 million years ago. The first part of the brain to evolve in primitive forms of life was all about sensing and sniffing out danger – essential to survival.[1]

Unfortunately for the earthworm, curling up or wriggling away are the only options it has for responding to threats to its life.

In response to this problem, around 500 million years ago, nature developed the brainstem – often known as the **reptilian or lizard brain** – to give creatures more responses to threat. When mammals came along some

300 million years later, their offspring didn't have much chance of survival without their parents' help. So nature evolved the **limbic system** or emotional brain. This enabled communication and bonding between offspring and their caregivers, which gave them a better chance of survival. Finally, around two or three million years ago, we developed the **cerebral cortex,** the thinking brain, which experts believe evolved to help us navigate complex social groups.

In summary, the human brain evolved to keep us safe, connected with others and equipped to live in society.

Fast-forward to around 200,000 years ago when our early human ancestors emerged. Neuropsychologist Dr Rick Hanson said our ancestors could make two kinds of mistakes.[2]

1. Thinking there **was** a tiger in the bushes when there wasn't one
2. Thinking there **wasn't** a tiger in the bushes when there was

Which mistake do you think we learned to repeat?

I'm hoping you chose the first one! The cost of the first mistake was needless anxiety, but the cost of the second could very likely be death.

Quite sensibly, we've evolved to make the first mistake over and over again. We've evolved to scan the world for threats, to look for the negative. As Hanson puts it, we've learned to "eat lunch, not be lunch".[3] If we'd been confident that there wasn't a wild animal lying in wait for us when there was, then the human race may have petered out a lot sooner.

In other words, we're perfectly designed to lack confidence.

Our brain has evolved to maximise our chances of survival and perpetuate the species.

And while we've come a long way from our primitive ancestors like the worm, we're still an emotional and sensory organ. We think, act and feel because of what our emotional radar system picks up in the world around us.

> We're perfectly designed to lack confidence.

Neuroscience tells us eight basic emotions drive our behaviour. Five help us avoid danger (fear, anger, disgust, shame and sadness), two move us towards people and action (excitement/joy and love) and one can take us either way (startle/surprise)[4].

Which is the easiest emotion to trigger? Fear. Because it's most closely connected to our survival.

Tigers at work

You might think that 200,000 years on, we don't have to deal with sabre-toothed tigers or neighbouring tribesmen threatening our life.

However, the modern-day equivalent is a volatile boss, an angry client, the threat of redundancy, the risk of looking stupid in the weekly leadership meeting, or the prospect of presenting in front of lots of Important People.

The problem is that our brain can't distinguish between man-eating tigers and, say, presenting to the board or sharing an unpalatable message with a team member.

And when our brain perceives a threat – real or imagined – our body reacts as if it's faced with a dangerous animal or warring tribesmen. It readies itself to run, fight or play dead, a physiological reaction commonly known as the "fight or flight" response, or sometimes as the "fight, flight or freeze" response.

When I started working with Niall, a senior finance manager, he'd been asked to sit on the leadership team. That meant he had to answer employee questions at monthly meetings in front of the whole company. He'd recently had an extremely stressful experience where he'd been asked a question in one of these meetings and his mind had gone blank. He didn't have a clue what to say.

When I dug deeper with Niall, we discovered that his heart started racing and his body tensed at the very moment he was put on the spot. He was also holding his breath.

You probably recognise these signs when you're in a situation that stresses you out. Like Niall, your heart races, you've got dry mouth, perhaps your hands or legs are shaking, and you may well be sweating. Your body is essentially preparing itself to be injured (think wild animals) and to make sure your arms, legs and shoulders have all the energy they need to run or fight. Your heart beats faster, pushing blood to your muscles and other vital organs, your breathing becomes more rapid to maximise oxygen intake, and perspiration kicks in to help you regulate your body temperature (not a good look when you're presenting).

When our ancestors didn't have the option to run or fight, they played dead. Essentially, this meant holding very still and not breathing, which explains Niall's response.

Added to this, when fear takes over, a part of our brain called the amygdala kicks off and short-circuits our pre-frontal cortex.[5] The brain shuts off the cortical networks involved in thinking creatively or strategically – anything that will get in the way of survival. When faced with a threat, our ancestors didn't need smart thinking – they just needed to survive. So forgetting what you were going to say is a common and embarrassing symptom.

None of which is good news when you're trying to get on with your job.

Our brain is very primitive...

Even though we live in a much safer world than our early human ancestors, our brains haven't adjusted. Our brain's structure is much the same as when our species, *homo sapiens*, emerged about 200,000 years ago. As physician and neuroscientist, Dr Alan Watkins puts it, *"We have 200,000-year-old software, and we've never had an upgrade."*[6]

Niall's responses made perfect sense for our ancestors, but aren't so useful in our lives today. It's as though our brain is in a virtual reality where presenting to the board is transformed into an angry, hungry bear.

...and very clever

> *"There is circuitry in the brain to ensure we not only learn what to be afraid of, but to never ever forget it."*
> – The Fear-Free Organisation[7]

At birth, we're only genetically prepared to be afraid of loud noises, heights and maybe dangerous animals such as snakes, spiders, tigers and bears.[8]

However, the brain is only partially formed at that stage and, as we grow up, fear plays a key part in developing survival strategies in response to our experiences. For example, if your Dad had a bit of temper, you may have adopted an approach of trying your best to keep him happy so he didn't get angry with you.

The problem is that strategies like these become ingrained patterns of behaviour to which we default under pressure. They are sometimes known as conditioned tendencies. So if you learned to avoid making your Dad angry by finding ways of appeasing him, a volatile boss will likely trigger the same behavioural response.[9]

It's like your brain remembering when you put your hand on a hot stove (for example, your Dad getting angry with you). It sees another hot stove (your agitated boss) and goes into action. It's as though your brain's saying to your body: "Hot stove alert! Trigger safety procedure!"

> It's as though your brain's saying to your body: "Hot stove alert! Trigger safety procedure!"

Each of us has developed our own unique survival strategy dependent on the experiences that have shaped us. These strategies mimic the different aspects of the fight or flight response.

Of course, if we get scared in a work situation – such as presenting to the leadership team – it's not appropriate to run out of the room or get into a fight with someone or lie down on the floor and pretend you're dead. That would be a bit weird.

Instead, we have different strategies to either move away from a perceived threat (flight), move against it (fight) or, like Niall, freeze (play dead). A fourth, uniquely human response involves "appeasing" or moving towards the source of the threat. This is about placating another person by saying or doing what will make them feel better and is often known as people-pleasing.

My experience from coaching hundreds of managers and leaders is that fear and lack of confidence typically manifest as either moving away from (flight) or moving towards (appease). And the related behaviours that I see most often are perfectionism, people-pleasing and procrastination.

Let me introduce you to three characters to bring these behaviours to life. They are fictional but bear a resemblance to many individuals I've worked with over the years.

	Conditioned Tendencies	Associated Behaviours
fight	move against	challenge, intimidate
flight	move away	avoid, procrastinate
freeze	play dead	mind goes blank
appease	move towards	people-please, perfect

Figure 2: Conditioned tendencies table

Perfectionist Phil

Phil has just been promoted to Financial Director in a charity. He's facing demands from all directions – his team, his colleagues and, not least, his CEO, who is relatively new to the organisation. He's on Phil's back all the time and is clearly anxious to look good in front of the board.

Phil feels he has to do things by the book, which prevents him from delegating as much as he should. He's afraid that others won't deliver to his exacting standards and that will reflect badly on him. With so much on his plate, it's not surprising he feels overwhelmed.

If we go back to when he was growing up, Phil was a high performer at school. However, nothing ever seemed to be good enough for his father, who was quick to criticise and never praised him. In Phil's desire to win his father and teachers' approval, his strategy was to push himself harder and aspire for perfection.

Fast-forward to the present day, and Phil is continually striving to keep up with the incredibly high expectations he has of himself. Not only is this exhausting, but he doesn't feel he can negotiate demands made by others because he's afraid people will think less of him.

Phil wants to make a meaningful impact in his new role, which means he needs to spend less time in the day-to-day and pay more attention to strategic priorities, but he's bogged down in dealing with other people's demands.

Procrastinating Pip

Pip is a marketing manager in her forties. Growing up, Pip's sister was a bit of a rebel, which led to a great deal of friction at home, particularly between her sister and her father. Pip found that being the Good Girl, the Good

Student and Not Rocking The Boat meant she kept her parents and teachers happy.

Fast-forward 30 years and Pip's desire to avoid conflict is playing out in a well-practised tendency to procrastinate. For example, she needs to have a conversation with an under-performing team member, but she's afraid of upsetting them, even though she's taking on their workload because they're not pulling their weight.

Pip has also been putting off talking to her manager about her career development, as she's afraid she'll receive negative feedback and be told she's not good enough for the next level.

Pip is a worrier. She worries about doing the right thing, and this holds her back from making decisions. She believes that if she keeps her head down and avoids friction, she will be approved and avoid criticism, just like when she was a child.

People-pleasing Pete

Pete is a senior manager leading a team of engineers. He's a Very Nice Man and super-accommodating.

His team members love him because he really cares about them. His colleagues appreciate him because he's always willing to help and volunteer to take on additional work.

But the truth is that Pete finds it difficult to say no because he's afraid of letting people down. This is having an impact on delivering his objectives. Although Pete manages the day-to-day operations, his line manager is frustrated that he isn't giving sufficient focus to strategic priorities and leading the change he's expected to.

Reflecting on his childhood, Pete was the youngest of four children. He noticed that, for some reason, his parents treated him as the favourite, and he believes that his tendency to prioritise other needs above his own tracks back to this time. By nature, he's a sensitive individual and his sense of guilt at being treated more favourably than his siblings plays out in his people-pleasing behaviour.

What about you?

- What do you identify with in the stories of Phil, Pip and Pete?
- What strategies have you developed to protect yourself from perceived threats?
- What key factors in your upbringing have shaped these strategies?

Our past shapes our present

Think back to the beginning of this chapter where you learned that human brains evolved first for safety, and then for connection. As mammals, we were, and are, dependent on our caregivers to look after us until we're old enough to look after ourselves.

Our caregivers are usually our parents. We need them to look after us and keep us safe from harm. Family members, teachers and other members of the community are also important influences in our development.[10]

From the moment we're born, we learn to adjust our behaviour if we sense any threat to our parents' love and approval and therefore their care for us. Like Phil, Pip and Pete, we develop strategies such as perfectionism, procrastination and people-pleasing to keep them onside as we grow up.

> These strategies may have served a purpose in our childhood, but they aren't so useful when we're grown-ups.

These strategies may have served a purpose in our childhood, but they aren't so useful when we're grown-ups with responsible jobs in charge of projects and people.

Imagine the organisation you work for as a tribe. For our ancestors, it was in their interests to belong to a tribe. It wouldn't have been safe to be on their own out on the savannah at the mercy of wild animals. So we've learned to do everything we can to avoid losing our place in the organisation we work within – our modern-day tribe – which means keeping our reputation and avoiding rejection.

It's no wonder that research indicates the three main fears in the workplace are fear of losing your job, fear of losing your job status and fear of unfair treatment at work.[11] The economic impact of the coronavirus can only be exacerbating those fears.

The Gender Factor

If you've got this far into this book, then I'm guessing that, whatever your gender, you grapple with a level of self-doubt. The research tells us that 30 per cent of men and 50 per cent of women lack confidence at work. What's more, there is a direct correlation between how confident we feel and whether we achieve our career ambitions.[12]

Regardless of gender, some of us are born more confident than others, with genetics determining 25-50 per cent of confidence depending on which neuroscientist you believe.[13]

The consensus in science seems to be that male and female brains are more alike than not, although research shows differences in brain structure impact confidence. Scientists are still unsure how many of our gender variations result from evolution and how many from experience, but some evolutionary drivers seem to be at play here.

The first is the fact that women have historically had less physical strength than men. Some years ago, I attended a talk by Austrian body language expert, Stefan Verra.[14] He explained that women needed to find different strategies to navigate threatening situations because they were unlikely to have been able to win a physical fight. Instead, they needed to communicate, "I accept you're stronger than me, so don't hurt me".

Women also developed a greater ability to read body language to better assess and respond to threatening situations. It turns out that the part of the brain called the hippocampus is more developed in women than men from birth. It enables women to link facial expressions to emotions – in other words, to empathise. Several studies indicate that women detect emotions, both negative and positive, better than men. This idea is linked to another crucial evolutionary driver for gender differences: women were primarily responsible for child-rearing.[15]

While both men and women have testosterone and oestrogen, men have more of the first and women more of the second. Oestrogen encourages bonding and connection, and contributes to a more risk-averse nature. This hormonal tendency towards caution makes sense, given that taking fewer risks meant women were more likely to survive and raise children to maturity. In other words, to perpetuate the human species.[16] On the other hand, testosterone encourages a focus on winning and demonstrating power that would historically have resulted in higher social status and access to the best resources.[17]

Certainly, these evolutionary differences indicate that our female ancestors were more likely to be the cautious worriers, scanning the horizon for threats, while their menfolk were out hunting. As we've explored, our brain is pretty primitive. It hasn't changed much since our early human ancestors appeared 200,000 years ago, which means that many modern-day women may be fighting their evolution more than men when it comes to cultivating confidence.

In each of the following chapters on how to master your mind, harness your body and speak your voice, I'll add a commentary on what's relevant to how and why lack of confidence shows up for women in particular. Look out for the Gender Factor box.

Let's get started

I promised to help you unlock three resources to unleash your leadership: your mind, your body and your voice. Let's start with how to Master your Mind.

FOUR

Master Your Mind

Do you have a voice in your head?

Is it a voice that says "They don't think you're up to this", "You're going to say something stupid", "What if you fail?"

If you're a bit bemused by my question, I'm not surprised. This Voice in Your Head is so insidious that it masquerades as bona fide thoughts in your mind. A bit like the cuckoo that lays eggs in other birds' nests and then tosses out the non-cuckoo eggs so the other birds will bring up the cuckoo's offspring.

In my experience, there are three particularly unhelpful roles this Voice plays:

Berating

This is when The Voice says things such as "You're not good enough" and "You're a failure". The word berate means to scold someone vehemently, which is exactly how it feels.

It's as though you're being told off by a bossy teacher. It's the voice often known as our Inner Critic.

When I met Kate, a senior manager in a Big Four accounting firm, it was as though someone with a whip was goading her on. She raced through her days trying to do everything faster and faster, literally running to meetings. She even slept on the sofa so she could work into the early hours and get up super-early to keep on top of her inbox.

Until we drew attention to it, she didn't realise there was a constant noise in her head. Like a loud radio channel that said, *"You're not good enough – you need to work harder and faster!"*

The Berating Voice is where your "shoulds", "have to's" and "oughts" live. For example, "I should know about X", "I have to work long hours to get the work done", "I ought to respond to emails from my manager quickly".

Ruminating

The Ruminating Voice is all about worry. It reminds you of everything you're worried you did wrong or might be doing wrong or that could go wrong – and the implications for what other people are thinking about you. It says things such as, "How am I going to get everything done?". Or "I fluffed my words in that presentation. What must people be thinking of me?" Or "What if someone asks me a question, and I don't know the answer?"

The word "ruminating" relates to how cows eat their food – after chewing and digesting, they regurgitate it to start the whole process all over again. Chewing the cud means chewing regurgitated food. The Ruminating Voice does what the cows do: going over and over worries ad infinitum, like a broken record.

For example, Poppy, a marketing manager, shared with me that she's often awake in the middle of the night worrying about the impact of something she did or said and stressing about what she needs to do tomorrow.

Extrapolating

This version of the Voice in your Head likes to draw conclusions about what you see or hear without checking it's true. It's also superb at mind-reading.

So it says things such as:

- "My colleagues will think I'm slacking if I leave the office at 5pm."
- "I can't ask my manager for a conversation about my career; they're too busy."
- "They were checking their phone during the meeting; they're obviously not interested."

This Voice is all about making assumptions – in other words, believing and accepting something to be true without proof. In my experience, it does an excellent job of stopping you from doing things that will make your life and work better, such as progressing your career, spending time with your children or pursuing a new business idea.

There's a good reason we make assumptions. Our brain is constantly processing so much sensory information that it's evolved to save energy by squeezing information together – a sort of mental shortcut.[1] From past experiences, we deduce patterns about how the world works, then apply these assumptions to new situations. For example, your brain draws a straight line between someone yawning and your presentation being a disaster, when that person might just have had a bad night's sleep.

When you throw in the fact that we've evolved to prioritise our safety, it makes sense that we make assumptions that protect us from perceived threats, like the risk of being unpopular with your colleagues or getting negative feedback from your manager.

Are you afraid of being found out?

Do you sometimes wonder why people can't see right through you? That sooner or later they're bound to find out that you're only masquerading as a successful professional – you really haven't got a clue what you're doing?

If so, you're not alone. Impostor Syndrome is a term coined in 1978 by clinical psychologists Pauline Clance and Suzanne Imes. It refers to high-achievers who live in persistent fear of being exposed as frauds, putting success down to luck, timing or what they perceive as others' incorrect assumption about their competence.[2]

Their original research focussed on women, but later research has shown that men are just as likely to feel like impostors.[3] A male friend confided that he frequently feels more like a 12-year-old schoolboy than a 50+-year-old CEO in charge of a multi-million-pound business.

While Impostor Syndrome is a catch-all term people use when experiencing self-doubt, it's just another variation of the Voice in your Head. The difference with this Voice is that it often kicks in when you're doing something you haven't done before – for example, responsibilities that come with a new job or promotion.

Its patter goes something like this: "Who do you think you are to be doing this? You haven't a clue what you're talking about. It won't be long before they find you out for the fraud you are."

If you have this voice, I suspect that, because you're so good at what you do (theoretically – I know you don't believe me!), you're adept at getting the job done without anyone having a clue that you feel this way.

The voice in your head isn't real

We're going to explore how you can deal with this Voice. However, before we do that, let's just call out something really important: *The voice in your head isn't real.* It's just a collection of negative thoughts generated by your brain as a consequence of evolving to be on the alert for threats in your environment.

Remember the example of the tiger in the bushes earlier in the book? It was better for our ancestors to think there **was** a tiger in the bushes when there wasn't, than to think there **wasn't** a tiger in the bushes when there was. The first error might lead to endless anxiety, but at least it kept us alive. Thoughts are an evolutionary legacy to keep you safe when your brain perceives a threat.

How many thoughts do you think we have each day? And what percentage do you think are negative?

Research puts the total figure somewhere between 12,000 and 60,000 thoughts a day with around 80 per cent of those being negative[4]. That's a lot of dark thoughts!

> The upshot is that 97 per cent of our worries are purely the product of unfounded pessimism.

What's even more interesting is that 95 per cent of those thoughts are, apparently, repeated from the day before. That makes total sense to me, as there are a few stock thoughts on regular repeat in my head including "You haven't done enough", "You need to do better", and "Are you sure you can do this?"

In another piece of research, scientists found 85 per cent of what we worry about never happens. Of the 15 per cent of worries that did happen, 79 per cent of the research subjects discovered they could handle the difficulty better than they anticipated, or learned a valuable lesson from the experience.[5]

The upshot is that 97 per cent of our worries are purely the product of unfounded pessimism.

Rick Hanson calls this our in-built negativity bias. We've evolved to continue to pay attention to perceived threats, even though they're rarely a matter of life and death anymore.

I love his analogy of the brain being Teflon for positive thoughts and Velcro for negative. We've evolved for anything negative to be given priority access to our brain. On the other hand, it takes at least several seconds of focussed attention to absorb a positive experience.[6]

A perfect example of this came up when I was coaching Sarah, a Head of Finance. She'd just received a 360 feedback exercise report to which more than 15 stakeholders had contributed. I'd reviewed the report before our meeting, and the feedback was excellent, both in terms of numerical ratings and written comments. When asked how she felt about it, Sarah immediately zoned in on one comment that said she could "perhaps have more confidence when presenting".

I needed Sarah to recognise and internalise the positive feedback she'd received before helping her assess and put into perspective the one, tentative comment made by just one person.

Perhaps you've had the experience of being in a performance review meeting where your manager was sharing everything you'd done well, and all you were listening out for was the "but"? The one thing you could have done differently? That's the negativity bias at play.

Unfortunately, the more attention we pay to our negative thoughts, the more we strengthen the neural pathways that carry them. It's a bit like turning a grassy donkey track into a motorway in your head.

What about you?

- What do you notice about the voice in your head? Is it berating, ruminating or extrapolating, or a mix of all three?

- What sort of things does it say? Given that 95 per cent of your thoughts are repeated from the day before, do you recognise a few familiar soundtracks?

- Is the voice always negative, or does it have anything positive to say?

The Gender Factor: Mind

Several studies have looked at differences in brain structure between men and women and what that may mean for our mental activity.

One particular piece of research conducted by psychiatrist Daniel Amen found that women's prefrontal cortex and limbic cortex are 30 per cent more active than men's. This indicates a disposition towards empathy, intuition, collaboration, self-control and appropriate worry. However, it also means that women are more vulnerable to anxiety and overthinking – in other words, they are more prone to worry.

Interestingly, it turns out both men and women have not one but two amygdalae, the part of our limbic brain that kicks off when it thinks we're in danger. One amygdala is associated with responding with action, the other with thought processes and memory. Whereas men tend to rely more on the first in the face of a threat, women tend to activate the second. Studies also show women activate their amygdalae more easily than men, suggesting women are more likely to form strong memories of negative events.

Two other pieces of data seem relevant here: there's a bit of the brain called the anterior cingulate cortex, often referred to as the worrywart centre because it helps us recognise errors and weigh up options, and this is larger in women.[7] Also, women produce 52 per cent less serotonin than men. That's the hormone that keeps anxiety under control.[8]

All these characteristics would have equipped our female ancestors to scan the horizon for threats as they raised their offspring. However, it does mean that many modern-day women may have more mental obstacles to overcome than men. Certainly, studies show that women are prone to underestimating their abilities, blaming themselves when things go wrong, rather than external factors, and holding back from going for opportunities where they don't feel they tick all the boxes.[9]

There's no-one else there

"We think we're experiencing reality but what we are really experiencing is our own thinking."
– Michael Neill

You've just read that your thoughts aren't facts, but an evolutionary legacy designed to keep you safe from harm. However, my hunch is that, while you get that theoretically, you may not be convinced. Surely that voice saying you're not good enough must be right? Isn't it risky to ignore it?

Let's emphasise that there is no-one else in your head. It's just you.

We are not our thoughts.

The problem is that the critical voice we hear in our head seems to speak with so much authority. It may even sound like real people in our lives – a critical parent, teachers at school, a bully.

However, we are not our thoughts: we are the thinker of our thoughts. As Michael Singer writes in *The Untethered Soul*, *"You are the one inside who notices the voice talking."*[10]

If you've ever experienced meditation, you may be familiar with the Noting technique.[11] When you become aware that your mind has wandered from focussing on the object of your meditation – often the breath – you are encouraged to note what it wandered to. For example, you might note "thinking" or "feeling" before returning to your breathing.

This awareness that your mind has wandered is the "you" that exists aside from the thought. Eckhart Tolle, spiritual teacher and author of *The Power of Now*, calls it the thinker.[12]

Master or slave?

The problem is that it's so easy for us to become caught up in our thoughts without even being aware that those thoughts are dictating what we feel and what we do – or, more often, don't do. We're at the mercy of negative thoughts that make us feel anxious and fearful, a slave to the voice in our head rather than the master of it. Remember Kate, who acted as though there was someone with a whip goading her on shouting, "Work harder! Work faster!"?

Tolle puts it like this, *"Not to be able to stop thinking is a dreadful affliction, but we don't realise this because almost everybody is suffering from it, so it is considered normal".*[13]

What would be possible if you could be the master of your mind rather than a slave to it? Perhaps you'd go for that promotion? Or speak up in the leadership meeting? Or leave your job?

Let's explore techniques that can help you.

Helpful or unhelpful?

Most of the negative thoughts we experience are unhelpful to us. For example, as I'm writing this book, all kind of thoughts keep coming up:

- "Who are you to think you can write a book?"
- "You've only written 8,000 words. How on earth are you going to get to 30,000?"
- "Why haven't you written more? What's wrong with you?"

If I hold any or all of these to be true, I haven't got much chance of getting the book done. (Though I'll admit that the amount of negative mental noise is slowing me down.)

When you become aware of thoughts like these, the first question to ask is, "Is this thought helpful or unhelpful?"

India, a sales manager, was finding some of her team members resistant to doing things differently. When we started working together, she said she didn't think they would ever change. Applying the "helpful or unhelpful thought?" test, India realised that this thought was extremely unhelpful because it meant she was giving up trying to influence the team. This, in turn, was creating a headache for her about how she achieved business objectives.

Once India realised her way of thinking was causing a roadblock and wasn't necessarily true, she decided to ask these individuals what was behind their resistance. She discovered they were afraid of change and what it would mean for them. No wonder they were holding on tightly to the status quo.

The 5Rs for managing unhelpful thoughts

I'd like to introduce you to a set of techniques for managing unhelpful thoughts that I've found have been helpful with my clients. Let's start with Reject.

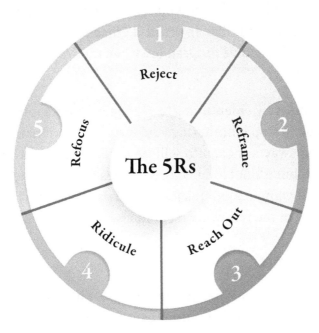

Figure 3: 5Rs model

1. Reject

If your thought isn't helpful, for example, "You haven't achieved much today" or "Nobody wants to hear what you have to say", then dismiss it. Decide not to entertain it. Don't give it the time of day.

Remember that your mind is just trying to keep you safe from harm, and it's not very good at distinguishing between threats. It mistakes the impact of sharing your opinion in a meeting with the appearance of a sabre-toothed tiger.

You might like to imagine you're putting the thought in the bin or deleting it like an email. Perhaps you can imagine the sound on a quiz programme when they don't guess the right answer.

Unfortunately, identifying a thought as unhelpful isn't enough to stop it bothering you. It's a bit like thinking that batting away a mosquito will be the last time you see or hear it, but it's not long before you hear that tell-tale high-pitched whine. So you may want to experiment with one or more of the following techniques.

2. Reframe

Reframing does what it says on the tin. Just as you'd put a picture you like into a new frame to show it at its best, reframing a thought is about seeing it from a more favourable perspective.

A recently promoted Director arrived at a coaching session very upset because the CEO had seemed determined to pick holes in an important report she'd prepared. And he did it in front of her peers. She interpreted the situation to mean that she wasn't good enough for the job. I helped her reframe her experience as, "The fact that the CEO engaged with the data means they're taking it seriously. They recruited me for this role because they rate me."

Other examples might be:

- Unhelpful thought: "I'm worried I won't know the answer."
- Reframe: "The value I bring is far more than what I know."
- Unhelpful thought: "I made a real mess of the interview."
- Reframe: "It was great practice for the next job I go for."

The same Director also used the next technique to check in with the CEO a couple of weeks later to determine how they felt she was doing in her new role.

3. Reach out

Reaching out is about testing out thoughts that bother you with other people rather than allowing them to go round and round in circles in your head. It's particularly helpful when we extrapolate meaning from what we experience –

in other words, make assumptions and hold them as true without evidence.

For example, Tami, a finance manager, was worried that her line manager had never given her feedback or talked about the possibility of her promotion. She assumed it was because he thought she wasn't up for it and was afraid that he would confirm her worst fears if she broached the topic.

After Tami and I had explored her worries, she realised she had no evidence for her negative thoughts about her performance and career prospects. The only way she could determine whether her thoughts were founded or not was to have a conversation with her line manager. When she eventually pinned him down, she was relieved to discover that he rated her highly but that it hadn't occurred to him to tell her!

The antidote to assumptions is curiosity. In situations where you feel disempowered or stuck, ask yourself:

1. What assumption(s) am I making here?
2. What evidence do I have for that assumption?
3. What would be possible without that assumption?
4. How can I test that assumption? For example, who can I reach out to for a conversation?

When the Director mentioned earlier reached out to the CEO, they gave her glowing feedback in stark contrast to the negative view she held about her performance.

4. Ridicule

The voice in your head can seem so real that it's challenging to see it as separate from you. It can be like a school bully. When they're persistently putting you down, you start to believe them.

The following exercise is a five-step process to help you isolate this Inner Critic and ridicule it. We want to take away its power. It's a bit like your friends ganging up on the school bully who's been bugging you and giving them a taste of their own medicine.

How to disarm your inner critic

1. Isolate it. *You are not your thoughts, and you are certainly not the Inner Critic in your head. The first step is to separate and contain the voice, a bit like caging a dangerous animal.*

Consider exactly where it is located in or around your head. (I know this sounds a bit weird but you might be surprised at how quickly you can answer this!) For example, your forehead? The back of your head? On your shoulder like a little gremlin? Responses to this question have been as specific as "behind my left ear" and "my right temple"!

2. Personify it. *The next thing we're going to do is to give this voice a character. What do you see in your mind's eye when you think of this voice? Don't be nice! My client Alex's inner critic was called Joe, and he imagined him as the Harbinger of Doom, dressed head to toe in black with a voice like Victor Meldrew. Another client imagines their Inner Critic as Angry*

Bird. Give the character a silly voice that makes you smile and makes it easier to dismiss the noise it's coming out with. I've had people say Bugs Bunny, Rumpole and Mickey Mouse. My favourite was "my mother on helium"!

3. Acknowledge it. *This is the tricky bit. Your Inner Critic has been an integral part of your brain's strategy to keep you safe. Find it in your heart to acknowledge how it has helped you – for example, driving your performance or ensuring you make the most out of life. Your Inner Critic may even still serve a purpose at times. Alex uses Joe to remind him of the downsides of a decision but makes sure to stand him down when Joe goes beyond his remit.*

4. Dismiss it. *This is the Really Important bit. When you become aware of your Inner Critic piping up, you're going to say "thanks, but no thanks" in whatever way works for you. You might say "Go away" (or a ruder version!), or "I don't need you, I've got this". Given that you're going to have to practise dismissing your Inner Critic every time it pops up (which will be A LOT), a simple "Shut up" may suffice.*

5. Overpower it. *When my husband, Bryan, and I first met, he joked that he was my "Number One Fan". He buoyed me up with words of encouragement and celebrated what went well for me – even coming to cheer me on at a tennis match. (He's still supportive, though, more than ten years on, a little less enthusiastic!)*

If you've got a "Number One Fan" in your life, that's great. However, it's no good having a cheerleader in your life if your Inner Critic cancels it out. You need to be your own Number

One Fan. Given being hard on ourselves comes so much more easily than being nice, you may need to play with ways of conjuring up a positive voice – or voices – inside your head.

Rick Hanson talks about appointing a "caring committee" in your head[14] while Matt Church suggests having an internal board of advisors.[15] These characters may exist in real life, like your best friend or your Dad, or they may be fictional. For example, Hanson's committee includes Gandalf from Lord of the Rings.

5. Refocus

My late mother used to say that the best way to deal with fractious children was to distract them. She'd say something like, "Look at that bird/bus/aeroplane." It never failed to work – they soon lost focus on whatever was bothering them, and their mood shifted almost immediately.

Negative thoughts are a bit like small children. We can pander to them and allow them to have their way, or we can shift our attention, choosing what we focus on in any one moment. George Lucas, of *Star Wars* fame, is quoted as saying, *"Always remember, your focus determines your reality."*

"Always remember, your focus determines your reality."

Here are two techniques for re-focussing.

Back to the present

Ruminative, negative thinking takes us away from the present to either dwell on the past or worry about the future. Earlier, I mentioned Eckhart Tolle, author of the best-seller *The Power of Now*. His message is that the present moment – the Now – is all we ever have. He maintains we can't have a problem in the present moment – we only create them in our thoughts.

> We can't have a problem in the present moment – we only create them in our thoughts.

I thought I was mindful, but, through Tolle's work, I realise how many problems and how much stress I create for myself by being "in my head", not in the present. When caught up in unhelpful thoughts, I've been practising dragging my attention back to the present moment. It's not easy, and it takes a lot of effort on a moment-by-moment basis – like trying to tether a hot air balloon in a gale. But it's worth it to feel calmer, less overwhelmed and more in perspective.

Try it now

- Bring your focus to this moment. What can you feel in your body? Maybe it's the sensation of your feet on the ground or tension in your shoulders.

- What can you see? Perhaps it's as simple as paying closer attention to the items on your desk or in the room you're in. If you're with other people, you might like to focus on what they're wearing.
- What can you hear? Listen for sounds in your immediate environment and further away.

Notice how you're feeling as a result of this short exercise. What's different?

Feed the positive

Just as we are highly skilled at focussing on the negative, we can build our capacity to focus on the positive.

As Shawn Achor shares in *The Happiness Advantage*, if you get into the habit of looking for positive things around you, your brain will learn to see more of them.[16] It's like when you buy a red Peugeot and then suddenly notice red Peugeots everywhere. Practising gratitude is a well-known technique for feeding the positive.[17]

Positive experiences take several seconds to be absorbed and often longer. It's no wonder that compliments and positive feedback bounce off us.

However, to do an effective job of building the positive neural pathways in your brain, you need to go a step further and **absorb** the positive. Neuroscience tells us that negative experiences immediately go into our body-brain, whereas positive experiences take several seconds to be absorbed and often longer.[18] It's no wonder that compliments and positive feedback bounce off us. So we need to focus on letting positive experiences soak in if we're going to offset our negativity bias. Rick Hanson calls it "taking in the good."[19]

Try it now. Recall a positive memory or a familiar place where you feel happy. It might be helpful to close your eyes. Mine is a woodland path where I often walk. Once you have it in your mind's eye, notice what you see, what you hear, what you feel, what you smell. Then dial up the experience as if you were turning up the volume on the radio. Stay with it for 20 seconds or so. When you're ready, open your eyes and notice how you feel. One client said, "I felt a wave of calmness flow from my skull to my feet". What about you?

I love this quote about feeding the positive, though I'm afraid I can't find the original source. *"Staying positive doesn't mean everything will turn out ok. Rather, it is knowing* **you** *will be ok no matter how things turn out."*

The 6th R: Relax

I want to call out an additional R here, and that's Relax. It may not appear to be a specific technique like the 5Rs, but it's pretty fundamental to your stress level and therefore to the noise in your head.

For example, when I feel tense and anxious, my head feels like a pressure cooker, full of thoughts about what I should be doing and where I'm falling short. Yet my mind is much quieter when I'm relaxed, after an afternoon sitting in the garden or a restful weekend. Things that were bothering me don't seem to matter so much anymore. Perhaps you notice the same thing?

> When you relax your body, you relax your mind.

When you relax your body, you relax your mind.

Relaxing, even for a few minutes, activates the parasympathetic nervous system. This is the other branch of the central nervous system from the sympathetic nervous system – the fight/flight response we've already discussed. The parasympathetic nervous system is often known as the rest and digest response because the heart rate slows down, the body refuels and repairs itself and stress hormones lower.

Whereas the fight/flight response is like the all-systems-go reaction to a fire alarm, the rest and digest response is where everyone's allowed back in the building, and it's back to business as usual.[20]

The problem is that we often postpone relaxation for holidays and weekends rather than consciously practising it as an everyday habit. And when we **do** relax, we may use stimulants such as alcohol or TV, which may feel comforting in the moment but aren't effective.

So how do you do it?

Back in the 1970s, cardiologist Herbert Benson came up with a technique called the physiological relaxation response.[21] It involves activating your rest and digest response using various mind and body techniques such as focussing on the breath, progressive muscle relaxation and mindful movements like tai chi and yoga.

I've been going to a weekly guided relaxation evening for a few years now which has continued virtually during Covid. I often arrive feeling wired, my head full of work. In the early days, I'd feel more relaxed by the end of the session, but still be awake. These days, it's pretty common for me to doze off within half an hour! Afterwards, I always feel calmer and more grounded because it takes me out of my busy mind and into my body.

"To go out of your mind at least once a day is tremendously important. By going out of your mind, you come to your senses."

Benson recommends spending at least 12-15 minutes once or twice a day to activate the relaxation response. However, when you haven't been doing it at all, even a few minutes will help educate your body to get better at relaxing. These words from Alan Watts [22] seem very apt, *"To go out of your mind at least once a day is tremendously important. By going out of your mind, you come to your senses."*

Try it now

Lie down on a bed or sofa. If you're worried about falling asleep, set the alarm for ten minutes – or even five if that's all you've got. Close your eyes and allow your breathing to slow and deepen. Notice any tension in your body and release it with each out-breath.

Many apps provide guided relaxation sessions if you find it challenging to do on your own. Try exploring Headspace, Calm or Heartmath.

What's next?

In the next chapter, we'll explore the relationship between your body and mind. I'll be sharing how to use your breath, posture and movement, not only to feel more calm and relaxed but also more courageous and confident.

FIVE

Harness Your Body

Welcome to your body!

We've spent a lot of time focussing on what's going on in your head. To be honest, we've been conditioned to privilege everything from the neck up. We often treat our body like a taxi that carries our head around and gets us from place to place.

If our body's lucky, we take it for a walk or a run now and then. We may even allow it to rest, in addition to some sleep every 24 hours (though we don't like to give it too much). And hell, it might even get a massage occasionally!

> We often treat our body like a taxi that carries our head around and gets us from place to place.

Come to your senses

The thing is, while your brain is at the centre of your nervous system, that doesn't mean it's in charge.

Remember the worm I mentioned earlier embodying nature's first attempt at a nervous system? Our body is first and foremost an emotional and sensory organ. Two-thirds of the work our "head-brain" does is about processing signals **from** our body. In other words, the worm could sense when it came up against, say, a rock and then use its muscles to change direction.

Here are a few interesting facts:

- **Your gut** operates largely independently of the brain in your head and is the only known part of the nervous system that can **override** messages from it. In fact, it sends nine times more information to your head-brain than the reverse.[1] Have you ever been asked, "What's your gut feel on this?"

- **Your heart** also has its own brain – around 40,000 neurons. The amygdala, the part of your brain that assesses danger, takes its lead from your heartbeat.[2] What's more, heart rate variability – the rhythm of your heart – is fundamental to the health of your entire nervous system.[3] You might have used the phrase "My heart's not in it" when something's not lighting you up.

- **The vagus nerve** is the linchpin of your nervous system with 80-90 per cent of its nerve fibres sending signals about the state of your body's organs, including your gut and heart, to your head-brain. It's like a communication super-highway. (More on this later in the chapter!)

In other words, your body is continually responding to your environment through your senses, sending messages for your head-brain to sort through. Professor Guy Claxton, author of *Intelligence in the Flesh*, wrote, "*The brain seems not to be the Chief Executive of the person, demanding reports and issuing edicts, so much as its Common Room. Where we used to say "the body **has** a brain" it now seems more accurate to say simply "the body **is** a brain"*".[4]

> 'Where we used to say "the body *has* a brain" it now seems more accurate to say simply "the body *is* a brain".'

If you want to stop fear and self-doubt hijacking your leadership and your career, then thinking your way to confidence isn't enough – you need to harness your body.

Intelligence isn't all in your head

Do you think being rational and logical is a Good Thing? Are you afraid of getting emotional at work in case you're considered irrational?

And yet how often have you tried to figure out a problem in your head and still can't make up your mind? It may have been about trying to recruit the right team member – or deciding whether to leave your job. You may even have gone as far as using a spreadsheet to rank criteria.

Neuroscientist and author David Eagleman shared a story that illustrates how crucial our body is to decision-making.[5] It's about a woman, brain-damaged in an accident. Injury to the part of her brain responsible for integrating signals from the body means she can't make the simplest of decisions. Her brain isn't able to read how her body **feels** about choices to help her prioritise, so she can't even choose between brands in a supermarket.

In other words, without accessing your emotions, you'll find it challenging to make decisions. The brain isn't just sending information **to** your body, but taking information **from** it to integrate with its logical function.

Recently, I had a coaching session by phone with a Director who was grappling with a dilemma. As I listened, it became clear that not only was he going round in circles, but he was working very hard at trying to figure out his problem. So I got curious about his posture. Sure enough, he said he was leaning forward, head in his hands, breath high and shallow – almost as though he was trying to squeeze the answer out of his head. Maybe you find yourself doing this too when you don't know what to do?

I invited him to adjust his posture so that he felt more relaxed and open. He sat back, put both his feet on the floor and took some deep breaths. I started by asking him to tune into his gut and see what it had to say. It took a few minutes before an insight popped up that surprised him. When I asked him the same thing about his heart, guess what came up? "My heart's not in it."

My client didn't walk away with the answer. However, he had greater clarity on the problem he was facing and realised he needed to allow himself more space to come to a decision. He also expressed a need to be "in his body" more often.

Hijack! When your body reacts before you do

Your body is often aware of things long before you're consciously aware of them. For example, have you found your leg shaking uncontrollably in a presentation when you didn't think you were anxious? Or perhaps you've had a tummy upset when you thought everything was fine?

Of course, sometimes you'll be very conscious you're nervous. Amy came to see me because she had to present the financials to the executive team every month and she was a quivering wreck before she'd even opened her mouth. As the meeting kicked off with her colleagues taking their turn to speak, her anxiety mounted as she knew it would be her turn soon. Her hands started shaking, and her breathing became shallow. When it was her time to present, she found herself babbling and unable to put the brakes on while her audience glazed over.

> It can feel as though your body's been taken over by an alien.

In some situations, you can be consumed by nerves without even knowing what triggered it. It can feel as though your body's been taken over by an alien. Anna, a senior manager in a consulting firm, shared an experience where she was chairing a meeting and suddenly felt sick. It was only after the event that she connected the sensation with the fact that a Partner had joined the meeting at the last minute. In hindsight, she realised she was afraid of saying something stupid and worried the Partner would think ill of her.

The body is like an elastic band – it defaults to instinct, especially when it senses a threat.[6] Even though the danger in Anna's case was potentially disappointing the Partner rather than being eaten, her body reacted in the same way. The body prepares to run, fight or play dead with all the physiological change that entails – heart beating faster, breathing becoming more rapid and the thinking part of the brain shutting down.

How to harness your body

The good news is that you can influence the way you think and feel through your breath, posture, and the way you move.

I find breath and posture are most important in my work with clients, so we'll start with those before talking about why movement matters.

And breathe...

Even though we take on average 20,000 breaths a day, it's mostly unconscious.[7] That's not great news given that your breath is pretty fundamental as to whether you feel stressed or not. The way you breathe has the power to either activate or deactivate your vagus nerve, the linchpin of your nervous system and essentially your inner superhighway between stress and calm.[8]

Vagus means wandering in Latin. The vagus nerve is known as "the wandering nerve" because it has multiple branches diverging from two thick stems rooted in the cerebellum and the brainstem that wander to the depths of your abdomen, touching your heart and most major organs on the way.

When the vagus nerve is stimulated, it slows your heart rate and lowers blood pressure by releasing a neurotransmitter called acetylcholine. The good news is that you can do it yourself by breathing properly. This means breathing from your diaphragm where your belly goes out when you breathe in and back in when you breathe out.

The bad news is that when the vagus nerve senses you're in danger – real or perceived – it disengages, exacerbating the physiological stress responses we've explored in this book. Like a drawbridge, it rises when sensing danger, and lowers when you're safe, or when you send it a message – by diaphragmatic breathing – that everything's ok.

What about you?

Where is your breath right now? When I ask this, my clients are often a bit perplexed. "My nose? My mouth? I'm not sure what you mean."

If you're also a bit confused by the question, here's another that might help. Does your breath feel quite high, in your throat or chest, or further down in your solar plexus or belly?

If your breath is quite shallow, you're in good company. Even though as babies we automatically breathe from our diaphragm, by the time we get to adulthood, we seldom breathe properly.[9]

Why don't we breathe properly?

Diaphragmatic breathing has many benefits – reducing stress, reducing blood pressure, lowering heart rate, improving core muscle stability, and improving sleep, cognition, immunity, mood, balance and digestion. So why is it elusive for so many of us?

- **Sitting around.** A sedentary lifestyle and lots of time spent on your computer and devices can make it difficult for you to breathe properly. If you're slumping, your diaphragm struggles to move up and down.[10] Over time, this can weaken your respiratory muscles, making it harder to breathe deeply.

- **Screen breathing.** Linda Stone coined the term "email apnoea" in 2008 following research that showed 80 per cent of her subjects held their breath or took shallow breaths when working on screens.[11]

- **Stress by stealth.** We've evolved to avoid danger. Even though we rarely face life and death situations anymore, the modern-day environment generates a constant stream of stressors that can trick your brain into thinking you're under threat – work pressures, a bulging inbox, demanding clients. It's become normal (though not natural) to be on a constant state of alert, which means your breathing becomes more shallow on an almost permanent basis.

- **Bad habits.** Even when you're not exposed to stressors, when you get into the habit of breathing from your chest rather than your diaphragm, this alone can trigger your fight/flight response and generate anxiety without apparent reason.[12]

Don't take a deep breath

We're often told to take a deep breath, but this isn't great advice. If your breath is high and you're not used to breathing from your diaphragm, you might end up taking an extra-big chest breath that causes even more tension. Not helpful.

Reading James Nestor's book, *Breath*, I've discovered the importance of carbon dioxide in transporting oxygen around our body[13]. If we breathe too heavily, we exhale too much carbon dioxide, which ultimately increases anxiety. Who knew?

> You should feel like you're on a rocking chair rather than on a bucking bronco.

While there is plenty to say about breathing, what emerges as most important in reducing stress and accessing calm is to slow down and deepen your breathing. Making your exhalation longer than your inhalation will activate your parasympathetic nervous system and start to calm you down. It's more important to breathe slowly, steadily and evenly into your diaphragm than to take big breaths. You should feel like you're on a rocking chair rather than on a bucking bronco.

Dormouse breathing

Here's how I help my clients to breathe better – first slower and then deeper. Take a minute to try it out.

Before you start, notice how you're feeling.

Make sure you're sitting or standing up straight and practise taking a few gentle breaths in through your nose and out through your mouth.

Place a hand on your belly and, as you continue to breathe, imagine you're breathing into your hand. You might like to visualise a dormouse asleep in your tummy. If you were watching a dormouse sleep, you'd probably notice a very slight rise in their belly. That's how gently I'd like you to breathe. What can also be helpful is imagining you're lowering a bucket into a deep well, a little at a time. With each breath, allow your breath to get just a little bit deeper.

Once you've got the hang of that, shift your attention to your body. Where are you feeling tension? Your shoulders? Your jaw? Your legs? You may find that this has already dissipated as you've been breathing, but see if you can release remaining areas of tension as you breathe out each time. For example, start by dropping your shoulders.

When you're ready, relax the focus on your breathing.

How are you feeling now?

Most people say they feel calm or calmer. What about you? Your head may feel less noisy and a little clearer. You probably feel as though you have more space and time.

How would it be to feel like this more often? The good news is that you can access this sense of calm in just ten seconds! Though I recommend that you also implement a daily relaxation habit (like the one shared in the last chapter) for around ten minutes, once or twice each day.

The not-so-good news is that it takes regular, conscious practise to embed any new habit – including breathing your way to calm. We'll talk more about how to do this later in the book.

Mary's story

Mary, a senior manager in a global accounting firm, is recently back from maternity leave. She's juggling a demanding role with mothering her 15-month-old daughter and is, unsurprisingly, exhausted.

*Mary brings a dilemma to our coaching session. She's been asked to go through the interview process for Director. It feels like too much to take on right now, but she's worried: What happens if she doesn't go for it? Will that be a Career-Limiting Move? On the other hand, how will she cope if she **does** go for it? Can she be a good parent as well as meeting expectations at work?*

I ask Mary to notice what's going on in her body. She's aware that her neck and shoulders are tense, and her breathing is shallow.

I invite her to sit back in her chair, feet flat on the floor, and to focus on her breath, gradually drawing it deeper into her abdomen while consciously releasing tension with each exhale.

After a few moments, I ask, "When you consider the dilemma you're facing, what's coming up for you now?" Without a second thought, Mary says, "Doing what makes me happy, not what makes other people happy." For her, that means staying in her current role for another year and creating a realistic career plan with her line manager.

Mary is astonished that this short exercise could have such an impact. "I'm amazed that it could change my whole way of thinking!" In our next session, Mary shares how she's been using breathing to manage herself during a busy project. "When I notice myself getting stressed, I've been leaving the room for a few moments and taking a few breaths. When I go back, I find I'm able to deal with demands more calmly, and I don't snap at my team."

The power of posture

Will you play along with me for a moment? Sit on a chair or sofa and slump in the best way you know how. You'll likely collapse your chest and hunch your shoulders. You might also want to cross your arms for full effect. Hold it for a moment or two. How do you feel right now? When I do this exercise in workshops or coaching, what is notable is what people **aren't** feeling: for example, confident, powerful, motivated.

Now sit – or stand – upright with both feet on the ground, shoulders back and your chest out. Imagine there's an invisible thread pulling you up from the crown of your head. How do you feel now? You're likely feeling stronger and more powerful.

When you think of your habitual posture, what do you notice? Do you tend to slump? Hunch? Cross your legs or arms?

How we hold our bodies – our posture – not only reflects *how we feel but also* impacts *how we feel.*

How we hold our bodies – our posture – not only *reflects* how we feel but also *impacts* how we feel.

The best-known research around this is from American social psychologist, Amy Cuddy.[14] She started from the premise that power results in greater access to resources, and that power tends to be associated with more expansive postures. Cuddy conducted a study where participants sat in either a high-power pose (an expansive posture that mimics Wonder Woman) or a low-power pose (leaning inward with legs crossed). They held this position for two minutes.

She found that holding high-power poses not only made people feel powerful, but it changed their body chemistry, increasing levels of testosterone and decreasing cortisol. I should point out that, while Cuddy's initial research was criticised for not being sufficiently robust, she conducted a second study that conclusively proved the link between expansive postures and feelings of power.

The Gender Factor: Body

In their book How Women Rise, women's leadership expert Sally Helgesen and top executive coach Marshall Goldsmith explore behaviours specific to women that could get in the way of their career success.[15]

They observed women minimise the amount of space they take up, whereas men tend to spread out. For example, in a meeting, women will often make themselves physically smaller, by crossing their legs, keeping their arms at their sides, keeping belongings close at hand, and making space for newcomers.

Unfortunately, in the modern-day workplace, making yourself small can have the effect of diminishing your impact and lowering your confidence. This makes complete sense given Amy Cuddy's research into the relationship between posture and power.

*The good news is that taking your space by assuming an expansive posture is proven not only to increase your **feeling** of power but also to increase your **impact** in the eyes of others.*[16]

Posture and performance

As well as showing that posture both reflects and impacts how we feel, research demonstrates a direct correlation between posture and performance. One study showed that maths students who sat up straight during an exam performed better than their counterparts who slumped.[17]

Daniel, a senior manager in a tech company, was finding his colleagues resistant to change. On calls, he often lost the will to keep trying to persuade them and found himself getting frustrated and zoning out. He also shared that he often had his feet up on his desk during these meetings (off-camera!).

Following our conversations, he practised a different posture on calls – sitting upright, facing forward, and with both feet on the ground. As well as working on his breathing, Daniel was more intentional about what he wanted to achieve in meetings and reported that he felt more focussed, present and in control.

Posture and your past

It's worth pointing out that it may not be as simple as sitting up straight. You may need to do some undoing. Have you ever noticed some people walk around hunched up as though they have the weight of the world on their shoulders? There's a concept called "armouring", which describes the action of contracting muscles to stifle emotion.[18] For example, can you recall what you do when you're trying to stop crying or laughing? It could be holding your breath, clamping your jaw or holding in your stomach. When we do this over and over again, it becomes chronic muscle tension.

One place I hold tension is in my jaw. Almost as soon as I relax it, it tightens up again. When I was about six, I was in the car with my parents when Dad wrapped the car around a lamp-post. We weren't travelling fast and emerged without a scratch. A shopkeeper offered us a cup of tea in her backroom. I remember that I couldn't stop crying – probably a shock reaction to the crash. Eventually, my mother told me in no uncertain terms to stop crying, which I did.

I got the clear message that crying incurred my mother's wrath and wasn't acceptable – or at least only in small doses. That may or may not have been when I first learned to use my jaw to repress emotion. One thing's for sure though, my mother's reaction to my crying is bound to have been (and continue to be) repeated the world over as parents will their children to be "good" whether that means being quiet, or controlling their emotions.

Play with your posture

What has this chapter brought up for you around your posture? You might want to reflect on the following questions before you move on to the next section.

- What's your habitual posture, particularly when working? Do you sit a lot? Are you prone to hunching over your desk? Or do you tend to cross your legs – or perhaps put your feet up on your desk like Daniel?

- Where do you notice that you hold tension in your body? The jaw, shoulders and abdomen are common places.

- How is your posture working for you? For example, does it help you feel energised, or would you like to make some adjustments?

It's also important to call out the impact of the coronavirus, which has seen many of us working from home. You've likely spent far more time sitting in front of a screen than before, and your home office set-up may also be far from ideal.

Awareness is the first and most important step, as we'll explore in the Three-Step Process. It might be that you start by noticing your posture during your day. You can then decide what changes you want to make to improve your confidence and impact.

Why movement matters

It's easy to forget that the brain evolved primarily to move.[19] Think back to the worm that needed to know to change direction when it hit a rock. Or the physical reaction when you accidentally touch a baking tray just out of the oven. We've evolved to move towards a resource (food) or away from danger (hungry bear).

You may be thinking that we've moved on a bit (excuse the pun) since our worm-like origins. However, movement remains fundamentally important to the way we think and feel.

One client came to a coaching session struggling with stress and fatigue. When we looked at her patterns of behaviour, it turned out she'd been sitting at her desk almost all day except for bathroom breaks and to grab a sandwich at lunchtime. And, as we explored earlier, sitting in front of a screen all day adversely affects breathing patterns.

> Movement remains fundamentally important to the way we think and feel.

Let's look at how you can use movement to shift your mood and thinking patterns, and what hacks can help you.

Move your mood

Since the onset of the pandemic, I've lost count of the number of times I've read advice that, if you're feeling a bit down or a bit stuck, go for a walk, even if it's just around the block.

Research shows there's a good reason for this.[20] As with any exercise, you're triggering the release of feel-good chemicals such as dopamine and endorphins, and reducing stress hormones. You're also impacting your posture and breathing patterns which, as you now know, are fundamental to managing your state of mind.

Moving in nature is even more beneficial. When you engage in "green exercise", your brain becomes calmer and exhibits few or no signs of anxiety.[21] Interestingly, a recent study shows that people who seek "awe" on their walks, rather than just treating it as exercise, experience more positive emotions over time and less stress.[22]

As I write this, it's mid-winter in the UK, and we're in our third national Covid lockdown. I'm fortunate to have the countryside on my doorstep, and my chosen form of daily exercise is a lunchtime hike. Yesterday, I walked out of the door to find the entire landscape sparkling white with frost, and a fine mist hanging over the hills. It was as though someone had sprinkled icing sugar over it and the powder was still settling.

It took my breath away, and the incredible landscape around me completely absorbed my attention. I often treat my daily exercise as a race to get my cardio in before getting back to my desk. Yesterday, I felt so much better for having directed my attention outwards and looked for awe rather than staying in my head, thinking about what I needed to do when I got back to work.

> Movement is good, and movement with your attention outwards is even better.

You might notice that this isn't just about movement. It also harks back to what we discussed in the "Master your mind" chapter about ways to refocus your attention and get out of your busy head. In other words, movement is good, and movement with your attention outwards is even better.

Even if you're in a built-up area, choose to look up when you go out for a stroll and get busy noticing the details of what's around you.

Shift your thinking

Do you ever find yourself sweating over a problem, only for a solution to pop into your head when you're having a shower or taking a walk?

In today's workplace, we can end up spending much time in front of a screen. When feeling under pressure, we tend to plough on with our work, believing that taking a break is slacking. Even when we're not working – or heaven forbid, allowing ourselves to be distracted from our work – then that may often be social media or a website.

The thing is, when you're focussed on a task, whether writing a report or scrolling through Facebook, you're using a part of your brain called the Executive Network. It's located in your prefrontal cortex, and is all about planning, focussing and executing.

However, another lesser-known part of your brain called the Default Network is so-called because it's the mode that the brain defaults to anytime it's not on-task. This network is responsible for light-bulb moments in the shower or out walking – or just looking out of the window. In the book *The Net and the Butterfly: The Art and Practice of Breakthrough Thinking*, the authors share a super metaphor for the relationship between these two networks.[23]

> Getting away from your desk and engaging in movement fuels your best thinking.

Your Executive sits in the front office of your mind and applies themselves to whatever project or problem is on your plate. When you take a break, whether going out for a sandwich or going to sleep, your Executive turns the lights off in the front office and takes a stroll to the deeper part of your brain. That's where there's a Genius Lounge full of beanbags and comfy chairs, sticky notes and different coloured pens and, importantly, lots of geniuses (think Leonardo da Vinci, Sherlock Holmes, Albert Einstein). The Executive turns the problem over to them and then leaves them to it while he or she does something else – nothing too demanding or it will take brainpower away from the Genius Lounge.

The Executive may check back in now and then to see what the Genius Lounge has come up with and make sure they're on track. Then comes the moment when the Executive is in the shower or out walking, and the Geniuses share what they've come up with (often known as an Aha or lightbulb moment) and hand it back to the Executive to make it happen.

This means that getting away from your desk and engaging in movement fuels your best thinking. And when you're out in nature, not focussing on anything particularly stimulating allows your mind to wander and reflect. This type of attention is referred to as soft fascination.[24]

Perfect conditions for your Genius Lounge to get busy.

Make yourself move

What about you? What do you notice about your mood and energy during the day? And how does that relate to your level of movement? When work revolves around a computer, it's easy to forget to move. The pandemic has meant even more time sitting in front of a screen as many of us have had to work from home.

A couple of years back, I bought a sit-stand desk. As I often work from home, I was conscious of the amount of sitting I was doing. Now with the desk, I stand far more than I sit and have more energy than I used to. When delivering webinars or participating in meetings, people comment on the difference standing makes to my impact. However, while many organisations have installed standing desks, standing instead of sitting isn't the complete solution either. The latest research says we need to be moving as much as possible for both physical and mental wellbeing.[25]

That means that, if you want to integrate movement into your day and improve how you think and feel, as well as your fitness, you'll need to be intentional about it.

Here are a few ideas:

- Set an alarm on your phone every half-hour to get up from your desk. Take the opportunity to stretch your legs and maybe fetch a glass of water.
- Schedule a recurrent meeting with yourself to exercise, ideally outdoors, whether that's before or after work or at lunchtime.
- When meeting with one other person, suggest talking by phone instead of video-conference so you can take the call on the move or outside.

Finally, challenge any belief you're holding that you're only working when you're chained to your desk!

What's next?

We've explored ways to master your mind and harness your body. Now we'll look at the third of the three resources for your journey: your voice.

SIX

Speak Your Voice

Fear has a lot to answer for

- **The Missing Conversation.** Are you avoiding confronting, say, a team member who's not pulling their weight because you're afraid you might upset them?
- **The Missing Request.** Perhaps you're holding back from asking your boss for additional resource because you're afraid they'll think you can't cope?
- **The Missing Voice in a Meeting.** Are you reluctant to share your idea or opinion with senior stakeholders because you're afraid you'll say something stupid?

When you think you can't speak up, it can feel like you're shouting inside, but nobody has a clue what's going on for you. But if you don't express yourself, you can't guarantee people will work it out. And this could leave you feeling frustrated and resentful and unable to influence what's important to you.

You can't expect what you don't communicate

The thing is, speaking up is when the rubber hits the road. To paraphrase author Chalmers Brothers, language isn't just a communication tool: it makes things happen.[1]

> You won't be heard unless you speak out.

So far, we've explored two of the three resources essential to your journey to unleash your leadership: mastering your mind and harnessing your body. While these will equip you to manage how you think, feel and act, you won't be heard unless you speak out.

In this chapter, I'm going to investigate what can get in the way of you speaking your voice and share some techniques to help you express yourself.

Let's start with a bit of detective work: The Cases of the Missing Conversation, the Missing Request and the Missing Voice in a Meeting.

The Case of the Missing Conversation

Many years ago working in a large corporate, I had a team member who could be described as challenging. We needed to have a conversation about the gap between her behaviour and my expectations – but I never took that opportunity.

I did my best to get on with her. I made copious notes about situations where her behaviour wasn't acceptable. I talked to her mentor and the HR manager.

To be fair, I wasn't the only one who hadn't confronted the issue – she had a long-standing reputation. However, I'll fully admit that I avoided having the conversations I needed to.

So why did I avoid it?

Fear of conflict

We explored earlier how humans are wired to maintain connection with others and to seek their approval and respect. That means that it's natural to feel anxious or fearful when there's a risk of damaging that connection. We want to avoid the possibility of provoking an emotional response such as anger or upset, which can make us feel as though we're in conflict.

In my case, I was afraid of not getting my message across in the right way. I was worried about how she'd respond (anger? recrimination?) and whether I could handle what came back. I was afraid of it getting nasty and that I'd only make things worse.

The Case of the Missing Request

Requests also require a conversation. However, this is where you're initiating a conversation to ask for something you want and need from someone. For example, you want to know your prospects for promotion or need more resource for your project, or you want to work one day a week from home.

Many of my coaching clients find making requests scary, and I think there are two main reasons: fear of being seen as weak and fear of rejection.

Fear of being seen as weak

Rae is an operations leader. Times are tough for her organisation, and redundancies are afoot. She's facing increasing demands from leadership with less resource to do the work. Rae feels she has no choice but to accept the additional work requests while also feeling pressure to protect her team as much as possible from the climate of uncertainty in the wider organisation.

She wants to say that she can't take on any more extra work without more resource, but she's afraid of pushing back in case she's seen as unable to cope. She's worried about what that will mean for how she's perceived, as she's in the pipeline for promotion to Director.

Not wanting to be seen as weak and not up to the job, Rae stays quiet, keeps her head down and continues to struggle.

Fear of rejection

Remember Tami, the finance manager who wanted promotion but had no idea how she was performing? She was afraid to ask her line manager because she thought they'd think she was too needy or pushy. And she was anxious that the feedback would be negative.

To be honest, even if she could summon the courage to initiate the conversation, she didn't know how she'd go about it. They didn't talk about stuff like that – it was only ever about the business.

The impact? Tami was wracked with doubt about whether she was up to the job and constantly read negative meanings into other people's behaviour. For example, when she wasn't invited to a meeting, she worried that it was the first step to getting rid of her.

The Case of the Missing Voice in a Meeting

I have a particularly vivid memory of being in an English class in my final year at school.

Our English teacher, Mrs Duffy, asked a question about interpreting a line in a Wordsworth poem. Lots of us raised our hands, and Mrs Duffy chose me with an air of, "Alison will get this right" (I was a bit academic at school).

But I didn't!

Mrs Duffy said, "No!" in a tone of surprised disappointment, and the other girls in my class looked at me with barely-disguised glee that I'd got something wrong. I felt embarrassed and exposed.

This is one of many experiences that honed my fear of reproach and criticism. I'm guessing you had similar experiences at school.

The thing is, doing well at school was about giving the right answer. You either got a tick or a cross. Even in college and university, you still had to make the right points – the ones the assessor was looking for – to get a good grade. You weren't (or not in my experience) given marks for your own interpretation.

Fear of losing your reputation

Fast-forward to adulthood, and one of the main fears my clients bring to coaching sessions is being afraid of saying something stupid or wrong, particularly in meetings with authority figures.

Their progression has often been grounded in technical expertise and knowing the answer. By the very nature of their success, they now find themselves in situations such as executive forums or meetings with potential new clients where the conversation goes beyond their subject matter expertise. They feel out of their depth and, if they don't feel confident in their knowledge, end up not saying anything.

Given our school experiences, it's hardly surprising we're afraid of being wrong. What's more, as we've explored, we've evolved to behave in a way that courts the approval of others, not rejection. We do everything we can to avoid being ousted from whatever tribe we're in, whether it's family, school or an organisation.

The Gender Factor: Voice

Earlier, I shared that women's brains have evolved to enable a greater capacity for empathy than men. Empathy can be a great strength in the workplace, but author Lois Frankel says it can mean women are over-sensitive to the mood of those around them, for example, a volatile boss or a frustrated team member.[2] This combination of empathy and a tendency to worry more can hold women back from having challenging conversations or pushing back on demands because they're worried about offending people.[3] The women I work with are often concerned that being direct will come across as too forceful.

In describing how women minimise their impact by taking up less physical space, Sally Helgesen and Marshall Goldsmith also observed how women do this through their language, using qualifiers such as "I'm sorry, but..." or "I just want to...". Women are more likely than men to downplay their certainty and acknowledge that others may hold different views.[4]

I've found this holds true in my coaching practice. One senior manager came to me because, whilst she was highly rated, her tendency to doubt her judgement and seek validation when

> *making significant decisions held her back from promotion to Director.*
>
> *On a positive note, using the techniques in this chapter, as well as managing unhelpful thoughts and harnessing your posture and breath, will help you speak your voice with impact – whatever your gender.*

How to speak your voice

All these fears we've named – fear of conflict, rejection, being seen as weak, losing your reputation – can conspire to stop you from initiating conversations, making requests or sharing your ideas and opinions. Instead, you can end up stewing in feelings of frustration or resentment while the people around you often remain oblivious to your suffering.

When you finally share what's on your mind, you may find yourself so worried about how your message will be received that you package it beyond recognition. It's like thinking that freshly squeezed orange juice is too strong and diluting it until it's more like orange squash.

There's something else going on here too: believing that you have a right to speak up, that your emotions – whether frustration, resentment or anger – are real and constitute a valid reason to express yourself.

The Three-Step Process I'll share in the next chapter will help you navigate stressful situations, including difficult conversations, making requests and speaking up in high-stake meetings.

Before we do that, there are three important aspects to speaking out, particularly when you're initiating conversations or making requests. These are Clarity, Conviction and Courage.

1. Get clarity

Worry is the enemy of clarity. When you're tied up in knots about how to say something and how it's going to land, what you genuinely want to say can get lost.

> Worry is the enemy of clarity.

I use two techniques to help my coaching clients get clear on what they want to say.

Spit it out!

First, I ask them to imagine that I'm the person they're thinking of having a conversation with – for example, a challenging team member or an uncollaborative peer. I reassure them that we're in a safe space, which means there will be no repercussions from what they say or how they say it. Then I just invite them to spit it out: to tell me, no holds barred, what they **really** want to say to this person.

I find this technique alone helps them articulate what they want to say and get in touch with what's bothering them. Often what they think sounds too blunt is actually clear and to the point.

You might remember Tami, the finance manager who was unsure of how she was perceived and what the future held for her, yet was afraid of asking her line manager for feedback. When she realised she needed to initiate a conversation, she didn't know where to start.

When I asked her to spit out what she wanted to say, imagining I was her line manager, she said without hesitation, "I want you to tell me whether or not I'm in line for a promotion and, if not, what I need to do about it."

You can try this with a friend, with your partner or even with a mirror. Or you can spit it out on paper. The important thing is not to worry about how it comes out to start with; you can finesse it later. (But don't finesse it too much – remember to keep the orange juice!)

Write it down

When you've got something important to get across, it's a valuable exercise to prepare what you want to say and in what order. It doesn't mean you need to script it word for word, though you may want to refer to your notes in the meeting itself.

The main reason for this is that you're almost guaranteed to get nervous when you're in the conversation. That may make it difficult for you to think clearly, and you may lose your cool. If you've done the preparation, it doesn't mean you won't get anxious, but you will feel a greater sense of control.

I think these words from SAS soldier Adam O'Connell, sum it up: *"At times of heightened action, we don't rise to the occasion, we fall to the level of preparedness."*

> "At times of heightened action, we don't rise to the occasion, we fall to the level of preparedness."

2. Have conviction

Knowing what you want to say matters, but what if you don't believe you have the right to say it? Conviction means having a strong belief or opinion about something. It's about feeling certain. When you doubt whether what you think and feel is important enough to express, it can get in the way of taking action – for example, calling a team member out on their behaviour. And if you act without conviction, you won't feel you're on solid ground.

Jane, a Director in a consulting firm, avoided confronting a direct report (let's call her Caroline) who was being uncollaborative and aggressive, and undermining her authority. A people-pleaser when under pressure, Jane often found herself apologising when they had crunchy interactions. She was trying to make things better, taking the blame for what wasn't working rather than attributing responsibility to Caroline.

First of all, I asked Jane, "What's your right to have a conversation with Caroline?"

We talked about her role as a line manager and Caroline's obligation to meet expectations, not only in meeting the numbers but also about how she went about her work, which included how she related to others. For Jane, having this conversation was also about taking a stand for her right to be respected as a human being, manager or not. It was a powerful insight for her to recognise that her feelings of frustration and hurt were real for her, and a valid reason to call out the impact of Caroline's behaviour.

Secondly, I asked Jane, "Where are you tolerating behaviour that isn't acceptable to you?"

One of the reasons Jane had been reluctant to confront Caroline was that Caroline's work quality was excellent, even though her communication and relationship skills weren't. Having got in touch with her right to take a stand with Caroline, Jane reeled off a list of unacceptable behaviours, with reference to the organisation's performance framework.

Thirdly, I asked Jane, "What's important to you about having this conversation? What is the cost of not saying anything? To you, to others, to your organisation?"

Jane said that if she didn't say anything, Caroline would continue to undermine her and Jane would continue to feel high stress levels in a toxic work environment. Caroline's unacceptable behaviour was also getting in the way of achieving business objectives that were dependent on collaborating across the business.

Affirming her right to have a conversation with Caroline and getting clear on what she wanted to say was the first step for Jane to confront her. We also worked with other techniques we've explored in this book to help her manage her nerves by mastering her mind and harnessing her body. The good news is that the conversation went much better than Jane had anticipated. Caroline recognised her destructive behaviours whilst Jane felt a new sense of empowerment.

Over to you

If you're vacillating over whether to initiate a conversation, ask yourself the following questions:

1. What is my right to have a conversation?
2. Where am I tolerating behaviour that isn't acceptable to me?
3. What's important to me about having this conversation? What is the cost of not saying anything? To me, to others, to my organisation?

3. Courage before confidence

You're clear on what you want to say, and you feel entitled to say it, yet you're afraid of the consequences of speaking up. Given everything we've explored about your fears, it's not surprising you're holding back.

However, you can't wait until you feel confident to act. First, you need to summon the strength to show up and speak up in situations that scare you: to take courage.

> "You can choose courage, or you can choose comfort. You cannot have both."

Research professor and author, Brené Brown, puts it like this: *"You can choose courage, or you can choose comfort. You cannot have both."*[5] In other words, when you avoid situations that you're afraid of, such as challenging conversations, you may avoid feeling discomfort, but you're compromising what's important to you.

The more you act in spite of fear and do things that make you feel uncomfortable, the more your comfort zone will expand, and the more confident you will feel. In other words, you need to do what scares you – with courage – to increase your confidence.

Remember Rae who felt she had no choice but to accept all the additional work asked of her and her team? Her turning point was realising that she **could** push back and be the gatekeeper of the demands flowing to her team rather than the middleman. She used the phrase needing "to put her Big Girl Pants on" to feel empowered to talk with her management. I think this is an excellent metaphor for courage. Pulling on your big pants is about raising yourself to your full height and embodying a feeling of resolve for what you need to do. The male equivalent is "to gird your loins" which has the same sense of preparing yourself mentally and physically.

What's next?

In the next chapter, I'll take you through a Three-Step Process that will help you use mind and body to embody the courage to show up in situations that you find challenging and achieve your desired outcomes.

SEVEN

A Three-Step Process

Fighting our evolution

You might be thinking, "Well, it's great having all these tools and techniques, but what happens when my nerves get the better of me?"

I hear you. As we've explored, when you're in a situation that you find stressful, your body-brain perceives danger and automatically swings into the survival mode that it's been practising since you were a child. For you, that might be clamming up (flight), throwing your toys out of the pram (fight) or going blank (freeze).

These behavioural responses are hardwired into you and have become habitual when you're triggered.

You are not hardwired. You can change.

The great news is that you can rewire these habitual behaviours.

> Your brain doesn't stop developing. It changes more often in your life than any other organ in your body.

We've discussed that the brain is relatively primitive – it's virtually the same model as the one our early human ancestors had 200,000 years ago – but also rather ingenious because it adapts to your experiences as you grow up. It can do this because it's only partially formed when you're born and is the most malleable organ in your body.

In other words, your brain doesn't stop developing. It changes more often in your life than any other organ in your body. This phenomenon is called neuroplasticity.[1]

Even better, **you** can change your brain by changing how you think and how you use your body so you can remain calm and in control. You have the power to make neuroplasticity happen!

How good is that?

It's like riding a bike

Did you learn to ride a bike when you were younger? Have you got on a bike again as an adult after a long gap and found you still knew how to do it without thinking? Or if you learned to play the piano, do you find you're still able to play some of the pieces you used to, even if you're a bit rusty?

This isn't muscle memory. It's the brain wiring behavioural patterns into our body-brains which then become habitual. New neural connections enable you to ride a bike proficiently, or play the piano with both hands doing different things at increasing levels of complexity.

If you imagine the neural pathways in your brain as a complex road system, the learning process is a bit like a country lane gradually growing into a motorway. Neurons that fire together wire together. That means we can change old ways of doing things and create new ones.

A Three-Step Process to unleash your leadership

It's great that we have the power to change the way we do things that aren't working for us, but it's not easy. In the same way that it's taken many years for unhelpful ways of thinking and behaving to become ingrained into you, it's going to take a bit of work to undo these and replace them with more helpful stuff.

I've developed a Three-Step Process which I find helps my clients reprogramme behaviours that aren't working for them:

1. Awareness
2. Design
3. Practice

Over the coming pages, I'll walk you through this process so that you can apply it to situations in your own life and work.

1. Awareness first

Do you remember Niall, the finance manager whose mind went blank when put on the spot? He wasn't aware of the sequence of events in his mind and body that got him to that point – he just knew he was paralysed by fear!

The first step in being able to change our habitual responses in situations like Niall's is awareness. We need to recognise when the fear response gets triggered and examine what's going on in our mind and body.

This sounds simple, but it really isn't!

Firstly, around 45 per cent of our everyday behaviour is habitual.[2] In other words, nearly half of what we do is on autopilot. There's a good reason for this. Our brains evolved to automate repeated processes that freed up space for us to be open to other opportunities to thrive.

> Around 45 per cent of our everyday behaviour is habitual.

You might recognise this from when you're driving on the motorway, maybe in the outside lane, and it's only when a car brakes ahead that you suddenly realise where you are and that you can't remember the last five miles of road. This is sometimes referred to as unconscious competence because your body-brain can perform a task without conscious attention.[3]

Secondly, if you pander to the negative thoughts that your brain so loves to generate, they may adversely impact your posture, breathing and mood. If you don't clock what's going on from the neck down, you may miss the Warning Signs that you're becoming stressed – for example, your shoulders rising to your ears or your breathing becoming shallow.

And finally, as we've explored, our physiological responses to perceived danger are very fast. In a situation that triggers our fear response, it can feel as though our body has been taken over by an alien and we have no control over it.

Be like David Attenborough

Suppose we want to understand what's going on in a situation like Niall's. We need the combined skills of a film editor and a naturalist (like David Attenborough) so that we can activate the slow-motion replay of the situation and zone in, moment by moment, to what's going on in our mind and body.

To help illustrate how the Three-Step Process works in practice, meet Rebecca, a senior manager in a professional services firm. When we started working together, she was nervous about speaking up in meetings. She shared a specific situation about being in a meeting with a Partner and a potential new client. As the client opportunity was in an area outside her zone of expertise, she felt really anxious and ended up leaving the meeting without having said anything.

When we activated a slow-motion replay and took a closer look, we discovered that:

- Her shoulders and abdomen were tensed up, and her legs tightly crossed.
- She felt as if she was holding her breath.
- All she could think was, "I don't have the right experience. I don't know what I'm talking about." The more she thought this, the more anxious she felt.

With the benefit of hindsight, Rebecca also realised her attention was almost entirely inwards. She was worried about what the Partner and potential client might be thinking of her and was painfully aware of how nervous she appeared. Her negativity bias was having a field day, and she was "in her head" rather than in the moment.

Awareness is a chicken and egg scenario. It could be that your body senses danger first, and that feeds your negative thought spiral. Or perhaps thinking negative thoughts triggers your physiological fear response. The main thing is to get insight into what happened so you can design something different (that's the next bit).

Your turn

Take a moment to think about a recent situation where you felt stressed or anxious and reflect on the following questions. It might have been a meeting, or a conversation, or even an email you received. It could be a situation you often face, such as presenting to the board, or something less frequent, such as handling an angry client.

Ask yourself:

- What was the situation?
- When did you notice you were becoming stressed/anxious? What was the trigger?
- What did you notice about this feeling? What would you call it? Anxiety? Fear? Where did you notice it in your body?

It can be useful to draw a stick figure and label it with your insights. The diagram will prompt you to think of your whole body. For example:

- What did you notice about your posture? Did you cross your legs or arms? Did you tense up anywhere? Did you lean forward or back?
- What happened to your breath? When you're stressed, your breath often becomes shallow, or you may hold it.
- What did you notice about your thoughts?

I know it's easy just to keep reading, but I encourage you to take the time to work through these questions before continuing to the next section.

Now we're moving to the second step in the process. Keep your notes to hand as we'll come back to them.

2. Design your behaviour

Awareness itself can be an Aha moment – or at least sufficient stimulus for conscious change. After her promotion, one Director discovered that the leaders she had put on a pedestal didn't always know what they were talking about. It felt like an unveiling of the truth behind the story she'd created that leaders were highly intelligent and knew all the answers. That insight alone gave her more confidence.

> If embodying confidence were as easy as saying, "I'll just be more confident," then you would have done it already.

However, for most of us – especially when it's a stressful situation – awareness isn't enough to change an unhelpful behaviour. If embodying confidence were as easy as saying, "I'll just be more confident," then you would have done it already, and you wouldn't need this book!

The keyword in that last paragraph is **embodying**. As we've explored throughout the book, your head isn't in charge – it works as a team with your body. In other words, changing how you think about something isn't going to be enough to make a difference without doing something different with your body. And doing something different with your body isn't going to be enough if you're still thinking negative thoughts.

We need to design a new behavioural strategy that supports what we want to achieve, whether presenting confidently in a leadership team meeting or giving feedback to an under-performing team member. This is where, with our film editor hat on, we watch the slow-motion replay and decide what we want to keep or change.

There are four key elements to zone in on:

- **Outcome:** What do you want to achieve in this situation? What do you want the other person/people to think, feel or do?
- **State:** What do you want to feel that will help you achieve your outcome? For example, confident, calm, forceful?
- **Assume the position:** What do you need to adjust in your posture and breath to help you feel this?
- **Hold that thought:** What thought(s) would be empowering for you to hold in this situation?

Let's return to Rebecca

I'll walk you through the process using Rebecca as an example.

Remember, she met with a potential new client and a Partner from her firm and was very nervous about speaking up. We'd discovered that her shoulders and abdomen were tensed up, she was crossing her legs tightly and felt like she was holding her breath. Plus she had repetitive thoughts of, "I don't have the right experience. I don't know what I'm talking about."

Here we go:

Outcome: Ultimately, she wanted the potential new client to decide to work with her firm. That meant she wanted them to feel she was credible and someone they would feel comfortable working with.

State: To achieve this, Rebecca wanted to feel and appear confident.

Assume the position: At this point in our session, I asked Rebecca to simulate the posture she had held in the meeting and notice how she was feeling. (Health warning: Even though it isn't the real thing, doing this can trigger anxiety!) I asked Rebecca how confident she felt on a scale of one to ten, and she rated herself a three.

I then asked her to adjust her posture to feel more confident. Immediately, she sat more upright and put her shoulders back. I also encouraged her to uncross her legs as having both feet on the floor helps with grounding and balance.

She noticed her breath was quite fast, so she took a few moments to draw her breath deeper into her abdomen, noticing and allowing tension to release each time she breathed out.

Hold that thought: The empowering thought that Rebecca wanted to hold was, "I bring a lot of experience, even if it's not in this particular area. What matters most is being fully present in the meeting and focussing on the client."

Rebecca and I explored what would help her be fully present rather than "in her head" in the meeting. Shifting attention outwards from our thoughts disrupts the negativity bias, that evolutionary legacy that conditioned us to scan the environment for threats, and look for the negative not the positive. For example, rather than dwelling on her perceived inadequacies in knowledge and experience, how could Rebecca shift her focus to what the client needed and how she could help **them**? What questions could she ask them to help her understand their challenges?

I also shared a brain hack to interrupt negative thinking, when she found herself thinking negative thoughts and feeling anxious. I suggested she set herself mini-challenges to focus her attention outwards. For example, concentrating on everything red in the room or paying close attention to what the client was wearing.

I asked Rebecca to sum up what she wanted to remember when the anxiety kicked in during meetings. For her, it was:

- **Open out.** This was a reminder to sit upright and put her shoulders back
- **Attention out.** Stay in the room and out of her head
- **Breathe!** It sounds obvious, but a reminder is useful for when your fight/flight response kicks in.

Your turn

We still need to consider the Extremely Important third step of this process – Practice. But before we do, I'd like you to go back to the situation you brought to mind when we talked about Awareness.

Imagine you're going to experience that identical situation in, say, a week's time and ponder the following questions. I recommend you return to your stick figure drawing and jot your notes on that.

- What is the outcome you want in this situation?
- Given the outcome you want, how do you want to feel? For example, confident, calm, forceful?
- Reflecting on your posture in the situation, what adjustments would help to embody this feeling?
- What about your breathing?

- What thought(s) would be empowering in this situation?

We'll look at how you can embed the behaviours you've identified once we've looked at the third and final step: Practice.

Are you turning the page before you've gone through the questions? I really want to help you conquer the demons that hijack your confidence, but you do need to do your part. Do please take a few moments to work through them.

3. Practice makes confidence

Mike, an IT Director, was struggling to contain his frustration with his team. This frustration often erupted in angry outbursts in team meetings. As you can imagine, this shut people down and his team was increasingly disengaged.

Mike wanted to embody calm so he would be more considered and empathetic in these situations. He discovered that the key was deepening his breathing before and during meetings, and sitting back rather than leaning forward.

When I asked him what would help him practise his new breathing habit, he said, "Oh, that's easy! I'll do it all the time". Sure enough, the first thing he said when we next met was, "Sorry, I haven't done the breathing."

Remember that habitual behavioural patterns are wired into our bodies. If you don't practise the behaviour you've designed, your mind and body will default to instinct, especially if you're under pressure.

> Talented people aren't born – they practise.

There's been a lot of attention on practice in recent times. Matthew Syed, author and international table-tennis champion, puts the case in his book *Bounce* that talented people aren't born – they practise[4]. And not just any old practice, but *deliberate* practice.[5]

Top performers are clear on exactly what they want to improve. They dedicate specific and sustained effort to practising new skills, entailing endless repetition, and they keep upping the challenge. It's about the quality of practice, not the quantity. Malcolm Gladwell's 10,000 hours theory has come under much flak, though top performers still clock up plenty of hours.[6]

Much research on practice has been done with athletes and musicians, yet the same principles apply to life and leadership skills such as keeping calm under pressure, changing how we respond to requests or learning to say "no". We need to *practise* new habits so that they become natural.

In my work with managers and leaders, I help them create a practice bearing in mind three facets:

1. Little and often
2. Be specific
3. No pressure

1. Little and often

As I say to my clients, it's a Really Big Deal to make new habits. However, the good news is that Tiny is Good.[7] Frequency and repetition are more important than duration when teaching your body new ways of doing things.

> It's a Really Big Deal to make new habits.

Earlier, I talked about a senior manager called Daniel, who found himself zoning out of conversations when frustrated with his colleagues. Before each of his many calls during the day, Daniel committed to spending ten seconds taking a few deeper breaths.

Taking three belly breaths on the hour will be much more effective than a 30-minute breathing binge at the weekend. Or, if you want to increase your knowledge by upping your level of reading, try ten minutes every morning rather than blocking out two hours on Fridays.

The Three-Step Process: Alice's story

Alice was promoted to Director in an area outside her expertise. She was afraid of speaking up in executive forums because she didn't think she had the relevant expertise, and the stakes felt higher.

Awareness: *We discovered that, when she did speak up, she felt anxious, and her breathing became shallow. She spoke softly and avoided eye contact. Her over-riding thought was, "I don't want to look stupid." The impact was that she wasn't heard.*

Design: *When I asked what was important about her impact, we experimented with what it felt like to hold the thought, "I may or may not be right, and I'm entitled to have an opinion." She noticed a shift in confidence, and I asked her to adjust her posture to reflect this. She sat up straighter and made eye contact.*

Practice: *Alice committed to practising the new behaviour in low-stake meetings in the run-up to the next executive forum. When we next spoke, she had become increasingly confident through her practice, reinforced by positive feedback from senior stakeholders who complimented her on her compelling arguments.*

2. Be specific

Remember Mike and his assumption that making a habit of deep breathing would be easy? The first step is to be precise about the behaviour you're going to practise and when you're going to do it. This will increase the likelihood of doing it.[8]

For example, rather than saying "I'm going to breathe more", commit, like Daniel, to taking three belly breaths when the ping goes off for your next meeting.

Other examples could be:

- Stand up whenever I take a phone call
- Sit up straight, both feet on the ground, when a meeting starts
- When someone asks me for something, pause for a count of three before responding
- Schedule 15 minutes for reading at 11am every day
- Reach out to one person in my network every day straight after lunch.

3. No pressure

When you're under pressure – presenting to the board, for example – you may find yourself consumed by fear before you can do anything about it. So it's Really Important to practise your new habits in low-stake situations, where you feel safe and comfortable. In other words, at times when you're not anxious or afraid about what might happen. It might be in meetings with particular colleagues or with your team, or even with friends and family.

Let's return to Rebecca

Rebecca came up with key phrases to remember when her anxiety kicked in during meetings. Open out, Attention out and Breathe!

She was due to attend a further meeting with the potential new client in a couple of weeks' time. Bearing in mind the three steps, Rebecca committed to practising her new strategies before that meeting:

- **Little and often.** Every time she sat back down at her desk, Rebecca committed to taking three conscious breaths, checking her posture and adjusting if required – for example, sitting up straighter, opening her shoulders and putting her feet on the ground. She put a reminder post-it note on her laptop which said, "Breathe! Sit up!"
- **No pressure.** She felt safe and comfortable in her team's daily meetings, so these were perfect opportunities for practice.
- **Be specific.** At the beginning of these meetings, Rebecca committed to the same practices she'd been doing at her desk (three breaths, check and adjust posture). She also made a point of paying close attention to what her team members were wearing.

Success!

When Rebecca reported back, she'd successfully used the techniques to manage her mental, emotional and physical state in the next meeting with the potential client. What's more, she and the Partner had won the client's business despite her perceived lack of experience!

When she noticed her anxiety kicking in – which happened several times – she adjusted her posture and breath and made a concerted effort to focus on what the client was wearing to shift her attention outwards.

Your turn

Let's go back to the specific situation you've been bearing in mind through the Three-Step Process. In the last step, Design your behaviour, you thought about the outcome you'd like if it were to happen again soon, what adjustments you'd make to your posture and breathing, and what empowering thoughts you'd hold.

How could you practise the behaviours you've identified? Think about:

- What could you do little and often?
- What would make your practice really specific?
- What situations can you use to practise where you don't feel under pressure?

The Three-Step Process: Daniel's story

Daniel wanted to increase his leadership impact and be seen as ready for promotion to Director, but he struggled to influence intransigent colleagues.

Awareness: *Daniel found himself getting frustrated in meetings. He noticed a rising of energy in his body, and said he felt "hot under the collar". Often, Daniel reached the point where he'd had enough. He dealt with this by either turning away or leaving the room.*

Design: *Daniel wanted to feel more statesmanlike which, for him, meant feeling calm, in control and objective. We explored what adjustments he would make to his posture to capture this. He sat upright, faced forward and put both feet on the ground. Focussing on deepening his breathing helped him feel calmer. The thought he wanted to hold to help stand his ground was, "I'm clear on my objective."*

Practice: *Daniel committed to practising the posture in low-stake meetings and taking ten seconds before meetings to take a few deeper breaths. He reported that he felt more in control, present and better able to think on his feet. However, he found it hard to remember to do his breathing practice as he hadn't yet set up a cue to remind him. His action was to put a Post-it note on his laptop.*

Remembering to do it

It can be easy to forget new habits because they're not yet habitual! So it's a good idea to use cues to remind you. It might be one you create, such as putting a Post-it note on your laptop that says "Breathe" – or finding an existing habit that you can piggyback on. For example, every time you're waiting for the kettle to boil, notice where you're holding tension in your body and release it on your out-breath.

We can get immune to cues so you may need to change them up until the habit is established. It's easy for a Post-it note to become part of the furniture and we stop noticing it because it's not new anymore. If that happens and the habit isn't habitual yet, create a new cue.

Time for you to put it into action...

Make a list of situations that you find challenging or stressful where you'd like to get different results. These could be:

- Presenting to senior stakeholders or large audiences
- Responding to being put on the spot in a meeting
- Having a difficult conversation with an under-performing team member
- Pushing back on requests from your line manager, colleagues or team
- Keeping calm when you feel under pressure

- Being less reactive to emails
- Protecting time for strategic work.

Choose one situation that you want to work on to start with. Don't underestimate what a Big Deal it is to change even one behaviour, especially if your fight/flight response has anything to do with it.

Work through the questions in the Your Turn sections at the end of each of the Three Steps: Awareness, Design and Practice.

List two or three actions you're going to commit to. It might be that you're very aware of what's going on in the situation you've chosen and you're clear on what you want to design and practise. Or it might be that you need to be like David Attenborough and pay attention to your responses in a situation that triggers you before deciding what you want to change.

Afterword

Early in the book, I shared the story of Sam, an operations manager under pressure to restructure her team, yet paralysed by fear of failing.

A year on from starting work together, Sam said, "I've learned so much. Most importantly, I have confidence in myself and conviction in my judgement. I've made the step from being a "competent-but-a-bit-scared" manager to being a brave, progressive leader".

And I should add that she successfully executed the restructure. She continues to flourish as a respected leader in the business.

Sam truly unleashed her leadership.

This book has been about helping you to overcome the fear and self-doubt that can so often hold you back from achieving your goals. It's been about helping you unlock your potential to lead yourself and others in service of what matters to you. It's been about empowering and enabling you to unleash your leadership.

Like Sam, this isn't an overnight transformation. It's a journey to confident leadership that requires courage.

I've equipped you with the tools to unlock three resources to help you on your journey: your mind, body and voice.

> This isn't an overnight transformation. It's a journey to confident leadership that requires courage.

You now know that the Voice in your Head isn't real – it's just a collection of negative thoughts generated by your brain as a result of evolution.

You have techniques to manage the unhelpful thoughts you experience using the 5Rs: Reject, Reframe, Reach out, Ridicule and Refocus. I introduced a 6th R – Relax – as a reminder that you can't master your mind without harnessing your body. When you relax your body, you relax your mind.

We've explored how important your body is to how you think, feel and behave. You can now use your posture, breath and movement to feel calmer and more relaxed, as well as more courageous and confident.

You know you can't expect what you don't communicate. You're aware of the importance of getting clarity, having conviction and taking courage when initiating important conversations.

Finally, you have a Three-Step Process – Awareness, Design and Practice – to help navigate challenging situations, using your three resources: mind, body and voice.

Remember...

You have everything you need to be successful and fulfilled. The resources we've talked about? They've always been there, but you might not have accessed them until now.

Yes, you're going to need to practise using them, which will take awareness and perseverance.

Yet what I know for sure is: *You've got this.*

References

Chapter 1

1. Gallie, D., Felstead, A., Green F. & Hande, I. (2012). *Fear at work in Britain: First findings from the UK Skills and Employment Survey, 2012.* https://www.cardiff.ac.uk/__data/assets/pdf_file/0003/118641/4.-Fear-at-Work-Minireport.pdf

2. Westfall, C. (April 8, 2019). Leadership Survey: Over 77% Of CEOs Are Looking For These Two Critical Skills. *Forbes.* https://www.forbes.com/sites/chriswestfall/2019/04/08/leadership-survey-ceos-critical-skills/?sh=79beb3556d10

Chapter 2

1 Kay, K. & Shipman C. (2014). *The Confidence Code.* London: Harper Business.

2. *The Why Factor: Why Confidence Misleads Us.* (2019) BBC World Service, (21 May). https://www.bbc.co.uk/programmes/w3csytzh

3. Holmes, T. (August 22, 2019). How to become a great impostor. *The Conversation.* https://theconversation.com/how-to-become-a-great-impostor-98798

4. Institute of Leadership and Management. (2011). *Ambition and gender at work.* https://www.institutelm.com/resourceLibrary/ambition-and-gender-at-work.html

5. Mayer, D.M. (October 8, 2018). How men get penalized for straying from masculine norms. *Harvard Business Review.* https://hbr.org/2018/10/how-men-get-penalized-for-straying-from-masculine-norms

6. Campbell, J. (1949). *The Hero with a Thousand Faces.* New York, NY: Pantheon Press.

7. Masterclass. (November 8, 2020). *Writing 101: What Is the Hero's Journey? 2 Hero's Journey Examples in Film.* https://www.masterclass.com/articles/writing-101-what-is-the-heros-journey#3-basic-stages-of-the-heros-journey

Chapter 3

1. Brown, P., Kingsley, J., Paterson, S. (2015). *The Fear-Free Organisation: Vital insights from neuroscience to transform your business culture.* London: Kogan Page.

2. Hanson, R. (2013). *Hardwiring Happiness: How to reshape your brain and your life.* London: Penguin Random House.

3. Hanson, R. (2013). *Hardwiring Happiness: How to reshape your brain and your life.* London: Penguin Random House UK.

4. Brown. P., Kingsley, J., Paterson, S. (2015). *The Fear-Free Organisation: Vital insights from neuroscience to transform your business culture.* London: Kogan Page.

5. Brown. P., Kingsley, J., Paterson, S. (2015). *The Fear-Free Organisation: Vital insights from neuroscience to transform your business culture.* London: Kogan Page.

6. Watkins, A. (August 18, 2014). Control your physiology and improve your performance. *Training Journal.* https://www.trainingjournal.com/articles/feature/control-your-physiology-and-improve-your-performance

7. Brown. P., Kingsley, J., Paterson, S. (2015). *The Fear-Free Organisation: Vital insights from neuroscience to transform your business culture.* London: Kogan Page.

8. Brown. P., Kingsley, J., Paterson, S. (2015). *The Fear-Free Organisation: Vital insights from neuroscience to transform your business culture*. London: Kogan Page.

9. Richard Strozzi-Heckler (1984). *The Anatomy of Change: A way to move through life's transitions*. Berkeley, CA: North Atlantic Books.

10. Strozzi Institute. (August 7, 2012). "Sites of Shaping" with Staci Haines. [Video]. YouTube. https://www.youtube.com/watch?v=GeocLj5r3Wo

11. Gallie, D., Felstead, A., Green F. & Hande, I. (2012). *Fear at work in Britain: First findings from the UK Skills and Employment Survey, 2012*. https://www.cardiff.ac.uk/__data/assets/pdf_file/0003/118641/4.-Fear-at-Work-Minireport.pdf

12. Institute of Leadership and Management. (2011). *Ambition and Gender Report*. https://www.institutelm.com/resourceLibrary/ambition-and-gender-at-work.html

13. Kay, K. & Shipman C. (2014). *The Confidence Code*. London: Harper Business.

14. Stefan Verra. https://www.stefanverra.com/en/

15. Hampson, E., Anders, S. & Mullin, L. (2006). A female advantage in the recognition of emotional facial expressions: Test of an evolutionary hypothesis. *Evolution and Human Behavior 27*(6):401-416. DOI: 10.1016/j.evolhumbehav.2006.05.002https://www.researchgate.net/publication/228345052_A_female_advantage_in_the_recognition_of_emotional_facial_expressions_Test_of_an_evolutionary_hypothesis

16. Barber, N. (December 18, 2012). Why women worry more. *Psychology Today*. https://www.psychologytoday.com/gb/blog/the-human-beast/201212/why-women-worry-more

17. Pawlowski, B. & Atwal, R. (2008). Sex differences in everyday risk-taking behaviour in humans. *Evolutionary Psychology* www.epjournal.net – 2008.6(1): 29-42.

Chapter 4

1. Han, F. (September 1, 2010). How the brain saves energy: the neural thermostat. *Yale Scientific*. https://www.yalescientific. org/2010/09/how-the-brain-saves-energy-the-neural-thermostat/

2. Jarrett, C. (May, 2010). Feeling like a fraud. *The Psychologist*. https://thepsychologist.bps.org.uk/volume-23/edition-5/ feeling-fraud

3. Jarrett, C. (May, 2010). Feeling like a fraud. *The Psychologist*. https://thepsychologist.bps.org.uk/volume-23/edition-5/ feeling-fraud

4. Antanaityte, N. Mind matters: How to have effortlessly more positive thoughts. *TLEX Institute*. https://tlexinstitute.com/ how-to-effortlessly-have-more-positive-thoughts/

5. Goewey, D.J. (August 25, 2015). 85 per cent of what we worry about never happens. *Huffpost*. https://www.huffpost.com/ entry/85-of-what-we-worry-about_b_8028368.

6. Hanson, R. (2013). *Hardwiring Happiness: How to reshape your brain and your life*. London: Penguin Random House UK.

7. Kay, K. & Shipman C. (2014). *The Confidence Code*. London: Harper Business.

8. Stein, R. (May 17, 1997). Study Finds Serotonin Production In Women Much Less Than In Men. *The Spokesman-Review*. https://www.spokesman.com/stories/1997/may/17/study-finds-serotonin-production-in-women-much/

9. Kay, K. & Shipman C. (2014). *The Confidence Code*. London: Harper Business.

10. Singer, M. A. (2013). *The Untethered Soul: The journey beyond yourself*. Oakland, CA: New Harbinger Publications.

11. Puddicombe, A. (July 18, 2017). *What the Noting Technique is, and how to take advantage of it.* [Blog] https://www.headspace.com/blog/2017/07/18/noting-technique-take-advantage/

12. Tolle, E. (1997). *The Power of Now: A guide to spiritual enlightenment.* Vancouver, Canada: Namaste Publishing.

13. Tolle, E. (1997). *The Power of Now: A guide to spiritual enlightenment.* Vancouver, Canada: Namaste Publishing.

14. Hanson, R. (2018). *Resilient: 12 Tools for transforming everyday experiences into lasting happiness.* London, UK: Penguin Random House.

15. Matt Church. https://www.mattchurch.com/

16. Achor, S. (2010). *The Happiness Advantage.* New York, NY: Random House.

17. Emmons, R. (November 16, 2010). Why gratitude is good. *Greater Good Magazine.* https://greatergood.berkeley.edu/article/item/why_gratitude_is_good

18. Hanson, R. (2013). *Hardwiring Happiness: How to reshape your brain and your life.* London, UK: Penguin Random House.

19. Hanson, R. (2011). *Just one thing: Developing a Buddha brain one simple practice at a time.* Oakland, CA: New Harbinger Publications.

20, McGonigal, K. (2013). *The Willpower Instinct: How self-control works, why it matters, and what you can do to get more of it.* New York: Avery.

21. Benson, H. (1975). *The Relaxation Response.* New York, NY: William Morrow, Harper Collins.

22. Alan Watts https://www.alanwatts.org/

Chapter 5

1. Blake, A. (2018) *Your Body is Your Brain: Leverage your somatic intelligence to find purpose, build resilience, deepen relationships and lead more powerfully.* Self-published.

2. Blake, A. (2018) *Your Body is Your Brain: Leverage your somatic intelligence to find purpose, build resilience, deepen relationships and lead more powerfully.* Self-published.

3. Rozman, D. (December 6, 2017). Let your heart talk to your brain. *Huffpost.* https://www.huffpost.com/entry/heart-wisdom_b_2615857

4. Claxton, G. (November 11, 2015). Intelligence in the flesh. *The Psychologist.* https://thepsychologist.bps.org.uk/intelligence-flesh

5. *The Brain with David Eagleman: How do I decide.* (2016). BBC Four. (17 September) https://www.bbc.co.uk/programmes/b07030n9

6. Harvard Health Publishing. Understanding the stress response. (July 6, 2020). *Harvard Medical School.* https://www.health.harvard.edu/staying-healthy/understanding-the-stress-response

7. Wikipedia. (2021). *Respiratory Rate.* Last modified February 6, 2021. https://en.wikipedia.org/wiki/Respiratory_rate

8. Bergland, C. (February 2, 2013). The neurobiology of grace under pressure. *Psychology Today.* https://www.psychologytoday.com/gb/blog/the-athletes-way/201302/the-neurobiology-grace-under-pressure

9. Nurse Linda (June 3, 2019). Breathing differences between children and adults. [Post] *Christopher and Dana Reeve Foundation.* https://www.christopherreeve.org/blog/life-after-paralysis/breathing-differences-between-children-and-adults

10. Dalton, S. (August 18, 2020). Breathe deeper to improve health and posture. [Post] *Healthline.* https://www.

healthline.com/health/breathe-deeper-improve-health-and-posture#breathingrate

11. Linda Stone (February, 2008). *Are you breathing? Do you have email apnea?* [Blog] https://lindastone.net/2014/11/24/are-you-breathing-do-you-have-email-apnea/

12. Rifkin, R. (2017). How shallow breathing affects your whole body. [Post] *Headspace.* https://www.headspace.com/blog/2017/08/15/shallow-breathing-whole-body/

13. Nestor, J. (2020). *Breath: The new science of a lost art.* London, UK: Penguin Life, Penguin Books.

14. Amy Cuddy. https://www.amycuddy.com/

15. Helgesen, S. & Goldsmith, M. (2019). *How Women Rise: Break the 12 Habits Holding You Back.* London: Random House Business Books.

16. Amy Cuddy. https://www.amycuddy.com/

17. San Francisco State University (August 3, 2018). Math with good posture can mean better scores. *Science Daily.* https://www.sciencedaily.com/releases/2018/08/180803160212.htm

18. Blake, A. (2018) *Your Body is Your Brain: Leverage your somatic intelligence to find purpose, build resilience, deepen relationships and lead more powerfully.* Self-published.

19. Wolpert, D. (July, 2011). *The real reason for brains.* [Video]. TEDGlobal 2011. https://www.ted.com/talks/daniel_wolpert_the_real_reason_for_brains?language=en

20. Greene, D. (August 12, 2019). How walking can boost your mood and reduce stress. *Thrive Global.* https://thriveglobal.com/stories/how-walking-can-boost-your-mood-and-reduce-stress/

21. Gladwell, V., Brown, D.K., Wood, C., Sandercock G.R. & Barton J.L. (January 3, 2013). The great outdoors: how a green exercise environment can benefit all. [Journal article] *Extreme Physiology*

and Medicine. https://www.ncbi.nlm.nih.gov/pmc/articles/PMC3710158/

22. Sturm, V. E., Datta, S., Roy, A. R. K., Sible, I. J., Kosik, E. L., Veziris, C. R., Chow, T. E., Morris, N. A., Neuhaus, J., Kramer, J. H., Miller, B. L., Holley, S. R., & Keltner, D. (2020). Big smile, small self: Awe walks promote prosocial positive emotions in older adults. [Journal article]. *APA PsycNet.* https://psycnet.apa.org/doiLanding?doi=10.1037 per cent2Femo0000876

23. Cabane, O.F. & Pollack, J. (2017). *The Net and the Butterfly: The Art and Practice of Breakthrough Thinking.* New York, NY: Portfolio.

24. Basu, J., Jason Duvall, J., Kaplan, R. (May 16, 2018). Attention Restoration Theory: Exploring the Role of Soft Fascination and Mental Bandwidth.[Journal article]. *Environment and Behavior.* https://journals.sagepub.com/doi/abs/10.1177/0013916518774400

25. Keyes, C. (February 6,2 019). Forget standing desks: to stay healthy, you've got to move all day. *The Guardian.* https://www.theguardian.com/us-news/2019/feb/06/exercise-health-move-all-day-standing-desk

Chapter 6

1. Brothers, C. (2005). *Language and the pursuit of happiness: a new foundation for designing your life, your relationships & your results.* Naples, FL: New Possibilities Press.

2. Frankel, L. (2004). *Nice Girls Don't Get The Corner Office: 101 unconscious mistakes women make that sabotage their careers.* New York, NY: Warner US.

3. Nolen-Hoeksema, S. (2003). *Women Who Think Too Much: How to break free of overthinking and reclaim your life.* New York, NY: Henry Holt & Company.

4. Tannen, D. (September-October, 1995). The Power of Talk: Who Gets Heard and Why. *Harvard Business Review.* https://hbr.org/1995/09/the-power-of-talk-who-gets-heard-and-why

5. Brené Brown. https://brenebrown.com/

Chapter 7

1. Brain Core Ohio. (2014). Dr Norman Doidge: The brain that changes itself. [Video]. YouTube. .https://www.youtube.com/watch?v=sK5lnv8mo-o

2. David T. Neal, Wendy Wood, Jeffrey M. Quinn (August 1, 2006). Habit: A Repeat Performance. *Current Directions in Psychological Science.* https://journals.sagepub.com/doi/abs/10.1111/j.1467-8721.2006.00435.x

3. Wikipedia (2021). *The four stages of competence.* Last modified January 16, 2021. https://en.wikipedia.org/wiki/Four_stages_of_competence

4. Syed, M. (2010). *Bounce: How Champions are Made.* London, UK: HarperCollins.

5. Ericsson, A. (2017). *Peak: How all of us can achieve extraordinary things.* London, UK. Vintage.

6. Ericsson, A. & Pool, R. (April 10, 2016). Malcolm Gladwell got us wrong: Our research was key to the 10,000-hour rule, but here's what got oversimplified. *Salon.* https://www.salon.com/2016/04/10/malcolm_gladwell_got_us_wrong_our_research_was_key_to_the_10000_hour_rule_but_heres_what_got_oversimplified/

7. Fogg, B.J. (2019). *Tiny Habits: The Small Changes that Change Everything.* London, UK: Virgin Books.

8. Blake, A. (2018) *Your Body is Your Brain: Leverage your somatic intelligence to find purpose, build resilience, deepen relationships and lead more powerfully.* Self-published.

About the Author

Alison Reid is an executive coach and speaker. She loves helping smart people believe in themselves so they can unleash their brilliance in the world.

She's on a mission to help professionals overcome the fear and self-doubt that can so often sabotage their success. A catalyst for clarity and courage, Alison helps experienced managers and executives focus on what matters, communicate with impact, and lead themselves and others to great results.

As the book title says, she helps them to worry less and achieve more.

As a coach, Alison is known for striking just the right balance between support and challenge, and insightful observations and powerful questions that get to the heart of the matter. All served with a generous dollop of humour. People quickly feel at ease with her, and participants in her programmes say she's an inspiring and motivational speaker.

An Oxford graduate, Alison had roles selling concert tickets, marketing magazines and selling washing powder for Procter & Gamble before finding her home developing leaders nearly 20 years ago. She works both with individuals, and organisations such as PricewaterhouseCoopers, Dentons, The Institute of Chartered Accountants, Bauer Media and Cisco.

Alison lives at the foot of well-known Box Hill in Surrey, England, with her husband, Bryan. She loves the outdoors and nature, whether it's a workout on the tennis court, attracting wildlife to her cottage garden or hiking in the countryside. She often bugs her husband to play chess and always has a novel on the go.

Find out more about Alison and how you can work with her at www.alisonreid.co.uk